Where Life Meets Love...
Nudges Toward God

By

W. Dale Stewart

Cover Art by: Sally Bomar

The Brence Group
Maryville, Missouri

Where Life Meets Love...
Nudges Toward God

by: W. Dale Stewart

ISBN# 978-0615852560

Copywrite 2013, W. Dale Stewart
All Rights Reserved

No portion of this work may be copied in any manner whatsoever without the written permission from the author, except in the case of brief quotations embodied in articles or reviews. However, the stories may be told with authorship credited.

Introduction

I remember a story I heard many years ago about a guest minister who shared a meal with a family. The young man had spoken in the morning worship service and was invited to the midday meal in the home of a family that belonged to the congregation. The family was not wealthy but was willing to share what they had. As the mother, the father and three children sat with their guest around the dinner table, a large bowl of hash was placed in the center next to a large basket of homemade biscuits. After the table-prayer was recited a large spoonful of the hash was dipped onto each plate. The meal was filled with conversation, smiles and teasing. At the meal's end, the young guest turned to the hostess and complimented her on the wonderful taste of the dish and asked for the recipe. On hearing the guest's request, the father of the family began to laugh. "Oh shoot," he said, "hash don't have no recipe. It just sorta accumulates!"

The stories and thoughts shared in these next few pages are like that hash. These are stories of the real people who have shared moments of their lives with me. My experiences with those lives have all nudged me to look and move closer to God. These are the men and women who have nudged me to think more deeply and broadly about life.

Any journey toward God is personal but not individual. The journey is personal in the way a nudge from a friend wanting to point out something or someone is personal. It is like the first school dance, in those moments when a shy boy or girl begins to wonder what the other is like but it takes the nudge of a friend to get them onto the dance floor together. The music may excite and the beauty of the other may invite but the nudge creates change. It is often the whispered voice that is most clearly heard and the gentle nudge that is most powerfully felt.

As stories of Jesus are remembered and retold, they seem most often to be simple nudges toward God. Those who heard his stories about farmers and servants, women and runaway children, turned cheeks and broken bread felt his nudge to look toward God. Those who walked beside him started their journey with a nudge.

Sometimes a nudge comes in a relationship. Sometimes it may come through an idea or thought. It may be felt while considering a shared belief.

My favorite punctuation is not a period, a comma or even an exclamation mark but "…" With those three little dots, I feel a nudge to look at something else and I am invited to let the story become my story. They mean that the story continues.

These are my nudges. Some may become a nudge for you to move just a little bit closer to God. What I believe is that every life includes its own nudges – moments where life meets love!

*The porch has fallen into splinters,
The storyteller has gone,
But the stories remain
And perhaps a nudge is
somewhere felt.*

A Simple Nudge

I sat at the meeting, fascinated by a story that was being told by a man sitting on the opposite end of the table from me. I was fascinated not by the story itself so much as the way it was introduced and told. I knew the story well and I knew word for word how the story would end. I knew because it was a story I told just two weeks earlier to a group of people that included the new storyteller. He introduced the story as one he had heard "a long time ago but didn't remember where."

As I listened to his telling of the story, he emphasized every high point, included every detail, and moved toward the conclusion with great enthusiasm. It had been my story, but in his hearing and re-telling of it, it was now his story.

Telling stories has been the richest way to share not just information but experience with one another. With story we attempt to move the portrait and landscape of experience that resides between our ears to a place between the ears of another. Any story that we experience becomes in our own way, our story. In a story, like an idea, poem, or work of art, we feel a nudge to look beyond that moment and place. In that way, a story does not have a "The End" written at the conclusion of the telling.

For several months, six o'clock in the morning would find three friends, Coby, Paul and Dale walking around the track that encircled the university football field. It was a time for exercise, but it was also a time for conversation. As the laps were counted off, we would begin to drift closer to the outer lanes of the track and closer to the exit gate. The problem was that by the time we were approaching the gate, the story I had begun to tell around the last curve might not have reached a stopping point. So, around the track for another lap we went. The timing of my storytelling, introduced with a "by the way" became the reason for a groan duet by my friends if I started a story after the final turn.

One evening I had gone out to dinner with my friend's family including his parents. After dinner, we had arrived at the front of the parents' house, but before they could open the car doors and get out, my friend put the car into gear and began to drive away. When we looked at him, questioning what he was doing, his reply with a grin was, "Well, Dale had begun to tell a story so I thought I better drive around the block for another lap!"

Some people think that a story has to make a point. I think that it should nudge a person to think something or do something, even if it's silly…

Where Life Meets Love

It was just sitting there. A black square but not really a square. An oval, maybe, but it certainly was not a circle. Perhaps it was unique like a snowflake, but there was no delicate beauty to it. There it perched with its other pepper companions atop a volcano of film-covered yolk, just sitting and waiting for something life changing to happen. So, the black speck with no particular form and shape and those of us who wondered what kind of form and shape we would become, waited.

Sometimes you find your entire being so focused on one seemingly insignificant thing and to try to explain it to someone observing your trance leaves them wondering about your need for medication.

When focus is interrupted by worn stoneware plates sliding onto glass top tables, the rest of the dining room comes back into view. Voices from every direction echo off rough pine walls creating a spider web of sound stretching across the room.

Why are these people here? Why am I here? It's Sunday morning. This is Easter Sunday. This is the day that people of even half-hearted faith, sometimes commitment and once-a-year church attendance show up in their local pew. The high holy day of Christians and the room set for eating has few spaces left as people enter and sit and commune. "Why here on Sunday morning?" is a question which requests – no, requires – an answer in a voice that sounds peculiarly like mine.

Even with almost every chair and booth filled, it was easy to notice a table at the back of the room and the figure of a solitary man. Harsh storms of living had carved deep ravines in the once soft landscape of his face. And, the look on his face was almost a snarl. Each waitress, questioning his comfort, coffee temperature or planned food order was met by the same look of displeasure or comment of complaint. Surrounded by life and sound, he retreated into memories of hurt. Even those paid to serve navigated around the room as far away from the man as possible.

As food platters slid into place beneath spoon and fork, the owner of the restaurant wound her way through the crowded room, smiling and speaking to the occupants of each table. Her journey led her toward the table where unhappiness sat and played with his food. The man looked up to watch the beauty with the long blonde hair approach and as the distance grew shorter, his expression grew softer. When she reached his table and stood over him, she bent down and said something heard only by him, lightly patted his shoulder and just before leaving, kissed him gently on his forehead. So little done and so much changed.

Surrounded by life and noise, feeling painfully alone, the man waited for a word whispered that spoke just to him, a gentle touch that pierced walls and a kiss that reminded him that love is an experience that is real.

On an Easter morning, surrounded by the noise of everyone else's life, a meal became a place where life met love...

Grand-Abba

There was no chalk-covered blackboard to be found on a wall. There were no desks arranged in straight lines. No bookshelves were stacked with books on history, English, math and science. No bell was ever heard, announcing the time to change rooms, go play, have lunch or go home. It was just a front porch attached to an old frame house but although it did not look like a classroom, it was the place that a lot of learning happened. The front porch had a concrete floor that had a peach tree growing up through a hole that was made just for that purpose. Two faded green metal chairs with freckles of rust sat looking out on the red dirt and grass of the small yard. Brick pillars held the roof and were not to be climbed on if any adults were watching. It was a special place for a grandson and a grandfather to share.

My mother's father was named Alphonso Brence. In the army he was called Al or A.L. since he had no middle name. But to everyone who knew him and especially his grandchildren, his name was "Fonce." That may seem like a strange name but it partnered perfectly with his wife, "Mokey" which was short for Mozell. Sitting on that porch with Fonce, made that time magical for me.

Those hours on the porch with Fonce were a time that imagination was set free and possibility reigned. He told stories about his time in the trenches of World War I and surviving the gas attacks. There were stories of herding cattle from west Texas onto railroad trains headed for Kansas City and the big city adventures of a young man from the country. I found myself sitting on the edge of excitement as he shared memories as a city Marshall and county Sheriff in Oklahoma during the days of prohibition, Bonnie and Clyde and Pretty Boy Floyd. He even had a scrapbook with photographs of moonshine stills that he discovered and arrests he made. He had been a carpenter and recalled houses that he had built and men with whom he had worked. Someone might say these were all just entertaining stories but they were also life nudges. I doubt that it is mere coincidence that as an adult, I moved to Kansas City and kept finding my way back even after living in many other places. I doubt that it was an accident that I spent several years in law enforcement.

Sometimes my conversations and experiences with Fonce gave evidence to simple "truths" by which he lived. It was not hard for me to know what was most important to him. When the three generations of the family would sit together for Sunday dinner at Fonce and Mokey's house, the meal almost always included fried chicken. As I enjoyed the meal, I began to notice that Fonce took only one piece of chicken. There was always enough for each of us to have more, but he stopped with one. During one of our front porch times,

I asked him why he never ate more than one piece. His answer was almost too simple, "One is enough." I believe for him that was true of more than just chicken. One house that he had built and lived in all his adult life, surrounded by family and friends, was enough. One woman with whom he shared his life for over sixty years filled with good and bad experiences, was enough. One church that he supported was enough. One God, in which he had faith and committed his life, was enough.

In one of his stories, he began to talk about the Ku Klux Klan, and as he did so his expression became more and more angry. I had never been sure what he thought about various races, having been brought up in the South, surrounded by cotton farms and being a man of his generation. His clearest definition of the white sheet-wearing members of the Klan was "a bunch of worthless cowards!" And, when he said "cowards" the word came out like he was spitting a bad taste from his mouth. He looked at me and said, "If you believe something, even stupid, have the courage to show your face!" He had no use for anyone that was so cowardly as to wear a mask.

While telling me about prohibition, he dropped in another little nudge of wisdom. "Something you learn in one place will help you somewhere else." He continued making his point with a story about helping federal law enforcement agents search a house looking for the hiding place filled with illegal liquor. Fonce said he just sat at the suspect's kitchen table watching the unsuccessful search and after everyone else had failed, he went directly to the hiding place behind a false wall. He said that what he learned as a carpenter helped him see the inconsistencies of the wall construction and that there were nails where there should have been none. What he learned doing one thing helped him do something else.

He told stories that nudged my life in certain directions. He shared simple truths that nudged my beliefs. And, as I grew older, we talked about serious things and shared the meanings of life experiences with one another.

In conversations that Jesus had with his "heavenly father" the address he often used was "Abba." It is a term of familiarity, closeness and open sharing. It is a term that implies clarity and understanding. It is a name of shared identity. In our culture of busyness and constant activity, of seeking and acquiring, of the importance of the immediate and now, where do we find Abba? Who shares the stories that help us know who we are and to what family we belong? Who nudges us to see something beyond and bigger? Who tells the stories, shares simple truths discovered in simply living and who invites us to consider life more deeply and more broadly? Who stands in that space between past and possibility, helping us reach into each one? I have known him and hope to be him. He is "Grand-Abba…"

The Sunday Slide

There was something strange about the concrete floor of the porch on the front of my grandparent's house in Oklahoma. At a quick glance it looked like most of the house fronts in the neighborhood. If you walked up close though you would notice something a little out of the ordinary. There was a peach tree growing out of the concrete.

The peach tree was not really growing out of the concrete floor but out of the ground and through the concrete floor. When the old wood floor of the porch was replaced with poured concrete, my grandmother wanted the porch to be wider and the peach tree was in the way. Since the tree still produced great peaches, the solution was to pour around the base of the tree and leave a hole for the tree trunk. So, a peach tree grew out of their front porch.

That tree created interesting conversations, as people would visit my grandparents and see the tree for the first time. It did continue to produce wonderful peaches. The tree also was the source of an overwhelming temptation. The trunk of the tree did not grow straight but instead grew at an angle. The base of the trunk, where it emerged from the concrete floor, was only two feet from the wall-size picture window of my grandparent's living room. The often-repeated and well-known family rule was to never climb the peach tree. I am sure that all of the grandchildren had heard the rule several times. I know that I had. But, sometimes rules are not as powerful as adventures.

One Sunday morning during a weekend visit to my grandparent's house, the warmth of spring made it a perfect day to wait outside on the porch while the rest of the family dressed for church. I was there, the tree was there, and no one else there. It was the perfect setting for a climb. Dressed in dark slacks, white shirt, a red clip-on tie and polished new leather shoes, I began my climb. The problem was the brand new shoes and the early morning dew that coated the sloped tree trunk. Almost to the place where the first branch provided a solid handhold, my fingers lost their grip on the slick bark. The soles of my shoes became as slippery as ice skates, and before I could stop gravity, I began my slide downward. The trip took about one second and ended with my rear end crashing through the glass picture window. There was no blood and there were no broken bones. From inside the house there were looks of surprise and relief followed by frustration and anger. Stuck halfway in and halfway out of the house, I sat bewildered, wondering whether to laugh or cry and fearing what was going to happened to me next. I knew that whatever came next would not be by accident but by the intention of displeased parents. At least my sisters and cousins thought it was funny!

It took enough time to make us almost late for church, but with everybody helping pick up pieces of glass and pieces of wooden window frames, the mess was cleaned up. My backside was already sore and embarrassed, so I suppose that is why my parents did not damage it further with punishment. However, the "talking to" I got along with the disappointment of my grandparents and endless teasing from my cousins were punishments enough.

Although everyone who was present for that memorable Sunday slide remembered the details of what happened, over the years the telling of the story finally ended. I remembered every detail and feeling that was a part of that morning and never attempted to climb the old peach tree again. When the bugs finally got the best of the old tree and my grandfather sawed it down, I suspect I was the only one that was thankful that the temptation was finally gone. As it was hauled out to the brush pile to be burned, I felt relieved that the last remnant of my poor choice was gone forever.

Several years after the tree was gone and with it the memory of the Sunday slide, that same group of now adult cousins sat in that living room. In the middle of the loud conversation one of the youngest let out a yelp that drew everyone's attention. She then displayed her finger with blood trickling down onto her jeans. She had innocently reached beneath the removable cushion on the sofa and was stabbed by a small shard of glass. The piece of glass had come from the window that was broken from a Sunday slide many years before. Just one small sliver of glass remained as a result of a poor choice that I had hoped had disappeared.

I was forgiven by my parents, whose rule I had broken, and my grandparents, whose comfort I had damaged. We had all moved on with life and into new life adventures. But I guess that sometimes pain can remain, even after the forgiveness…

The Cellar

Those that do not live in the Midwest, that is to say between the Mississippi River and the Rocky Mountains, may not know what a storm cellar is. Put very simply, it's a hole dug in the yard, usually lined with bricks or concrete walls, with a heavy door attached for closing when family and friends run down into it for protection against tornados.

In the side yard at the house on South Middle Street, the cellar was a place of protection. It was a place of storage for mother's vegetable canning. And, it was a place of mystery. The cellar was also a place for playing. It easily became a fort, a hideout, a castle and anything else the children could imagine. Furnished with an old folding cot and a small table with broken chairs, it was a place that sometimes welcomed a different sort of guest.

The heavy door that protected huddled occupants from the storm's wind and rain was left open during the hot days of summer to allow the cellar to dry out from the moisture that dampened the walls and bedding. Sometimes though, other creatures would find their way down into the cellar after the sun went down. A stray dog or cat was not nearly as challenging as the discovery of a squirrel or snake or skunk!

So, each night, just after the sun went down, someone had to go outside, crossing what seemed to miles of yard, in the dark to close the cellar door. Alone! That job fell to the oldest of the children, the one older than three other daughters and one son. It was not a job that anyone would volunteer to do. It had to be assigned and it was assigned to my mother. As she would tell the story, accompanied by her mother's nodding agreement, I could see every moment that she described.

Every evening, from early spring to late fall, when dark covered the neighborhood and the only light was from a moon so far away, my grandparent's oldest little girl would venture out of the house. Leaving the front door, she would slowly make her way around the house, keeping within arms reach of the walls until she stood directly across from the cellar opening. Shadows reached out to kidnap her and every tree limb and bush rustled a sound of warning. Inhaling as big of a breath as she could, she ran fearfully into that great expanse toward that cavern that in the daylight had been a place of fun but now held indescribable threats. Once reaching the cellar, she pushed with all her strength, and then turned to run back to the safety of house walls, into the light and arms of mother and father. She would be almost back to the house when she would hear the sound of the heavy door slamming down into place.

Every night, every journey into the dark, every encounter with the sounds ended in her mother's arms and in tears. As the little girl shared her fears knowing that each night of the summer would be the same, her mother promised her that the next night, she would show her daughter something that would take away all her fears.

When the next night came with the sun down and the cellar door up, the little girl looked at her mother's smile as her father announced that it was time for the daughter to do her job. As the little girl began to leave the house by the front door, her mother quietly caught her arm and pulled her back inside. The mother held her fingers to her lips, telling her daughter to be quiet as she nudged the little girl through the house to the back door. She motioned to her daughter to look out the door and pointed to the bushes at the corner of the house. Standing quietly in the shadows, in the same place that the little girl had seen every other night as a scary place, stood her father, waiting for his little girl to walk into the dark. Her father stood watch every night, unseen by his child.

For the little girl, who was frightened because she felt alone, the dark did not seem so dark anymore...

A Head Start Doesn't Always Help

I guess there are some things you learn in life at the right time and some things you learn moments too late. But even things you learn a little late can still be helpful to know for another time. Learning facts about parents can be like that. I once asked my mother why it was that she never talked much about her childhood and the things she did. Her reply sparked my curiosity. She simply said, "I don't want to give you any ideas." That may be so, but there was a little bit of parental history that would have been helpful for me to know.

There is a time in every little boy's life that he has to test the boundaries of his abilities. The most common way to do that testing is challenging the abilities of an older male, who is usually the father. When that moment comes, the information acquired and lesson learned can sometimes be painful. For most sons, we are irresistibly drawn to our pile of ego-stones and begin to build a personal Tower of Babel toward the domain of heaven.

I am not sure about what my age was, but I'm sure I was not as grown up as I thought. On a warm summer evening, my father and I had been in the front yard "playing catch." It was a way he and I often spent time together, enjoying the day and improving my baseball skills. After the last throw was made, he informed me that I had something to do.

To this day I don't remember what the job was but I do remember saying that I had no time or interest in doing the whatever right now. It was my moment of testing the boundaries. My father's response was "Yes, you are going to do it." My defiant stab into his manhood was, "No, I'm not!" His counter punch was, "Oh yes, you will." My thrust into his authority was, "You can't make me!" He assured me that he "could and would!" I then made that life changing challenge, "You have to catch me first!" I then turned toward the street and made my first steps into my father's history and my future.

When I began my journey away from my father, I was convinced that he was ancient and surely muscle had withered away from bone many years earlier. At my first stride, I was thirty feet in front of him. On my second step I could feel his breath on my neck. On my third and final stretch, I could feel his hand on my shoulder.

With my father now beside me, I shuffled along in the footprints of my poorly planned escape and into the house that now felt much more like a dungeon than a sanctuary. He escorted me to my bedroom cell and there administered to the best of my memory, the final spanking of many that had taken place on my calloused backside. After a brief sound of applause created by his hand and my bottom, he suggested strongly that I remain in the room for another minute. With the embarrassment of my first capture fresh in my mind, I agreed to his suggestion.

While I lay on my bed, trying to analyze where I went wrong, I heard my father rummaging through the drawers of my parent's bedroom across the hallway. In a few moments, he walked into my room again and without saying a single word, he tossed onto my bed three blue pieces of ribbon. In gold letters stamped on each one was "First Place – Oklahoma Track Meet." There was one ribbon for the 100-yard dash, one for the 220-yard dash and one for the 440-yard relay. My pained look asked, "Why haven't you told me?" His reply, "You didn't need to know until now." As I looked at the ribbons and then around the room, I could have sworn that I heard the sound of falling bricks once stacked in the shape of a tower.

Sometimes we learn things about fathers just a little at a time…

Three Piles On a Kitchen Table

Some of us grow up more fortunate than some others. I don't have a clue why, but I was a lucky one. When I say that I grew up fortunate that does not mean that I grew up with lots of stuff and that I always got everything I ever wanted. However, I never lacked for anything that I needed. When I recall that time of growing up in a small town in central Kansas, I could write for days making a list of things I am glad about.

At the time, I am sure that I did not have the faintest clue that this day of gratitude would arrive. Like most of my friends during our teenage years, I was taught and encouraged to the point of requirement to say "please and thank you" and to appreciate every day as something special. But, most of the time, there were ballgames to play, cars to drive, friends to enjoy and an occasional homework paper to finish before the very last second.

With so many things and people to recall and appreciate, it's difficult to look at just one. There is one remembered vision that is so clear I see it at the end of every month.

I was fortunate to be a part of a family that included a

man who always took his *yes* seriously. *Yes* is such an easy word to say. The lungs use very little effort and only minimal breath to push out the word, yet sometimes it may take great effort and all of life's breath to live it. He did not say *yes* casually when it was an answer to a request that presumed commitment. When he joined the church several years after marrying and fathering two daughters, he walked down the center aisle of the church initially to save the embarrassment of not accompanying his wife when she joined. His commitment may have begun out of embarrassment, but his *yes* to the minister standing in front of him was something he took seriously. It requires a serious *yes* to motivate a man to become a leader and even church treasurer for eighteen years.

There were a couple of additional serious *yes's* that made a difference in the way things were done by him and for the whole family. He said *yes* to his everyday after everyday responsibility to and for his family. He also said *yes* to the community in which he had chosen to live with that family.

Because of his experience with numbers in his work as a cashier-clerk for the Santa Fe Railroad, he was asked to be responsible for the church finances as the elected Treasurer. Because of the same observations by members of the local service club through which he supported his community, it was apparent to club members that he should be treasurer of that organization. Since someone was needed to keep an eye on family finances and group spending, there was never a question about who that someone would be.

The kitchen of our house flowed into a room that served as both the informal and formal dining room.

The eating area then opened into a family-living room where a television and upright piano presented the opportunity for hours of loud entertainment. But, during the last days of the month, that same house would undergo a transformation. The kitchen table that was the setting for food grabbed and meals shared became a workplace that would rival any Wall Street corner office.

During those hours at the end of the month, the television was left silent and none of the kids would dare to practice *Moon River* on the keys of the upright. Conversations were in whispers or better still, in the garage or front yard. Even if it was at the end of a panting hot July or August, the window air conditioner was left unplugged. It was time to "do the books."

The portrait of that scene for a teenager, with ballgames to play, cars to drive and friends to enjoy looked colorless and boring. On the last two days of the month, the same ritual was played out. When the evening supper was over, dishes were taken from table to sink. The old plastic tablecloth, the color of faded mustard, with a few remaining spots of old ketchup was wiped clean. It was then that we three kids knew, without being told, that it was time to stay out of the way.

He would sit down at the table after supper and in most instances he would be there until well after midnight. On the kitchen table in front of him were three piles of papers. In one pile was stacked his responsibility to his family. Another pile was filled with his responsibility for his community and friends. In the third pile was a collection of his responsibility to the church. But in fact, each pile was his *yes* to God.

Three piles on a kitchen table tell the story about a man who took his *yes* seriously...

The Big Black Lincoln

Growing up in a small county seat town in south central Kansas, a person can get to know something about almost everyone who lives there. There are very few secrets because so much of everybody's life just sits out in the driveway for the world to see. Each Sunday noontime, as the family made its way home from the First Christian Church, we would pass the house on the corner, at the top of Wheat's Hill, just a block past the hospital. While sitting in the back seat between two "much older" sisters, I would admire what sat in that driveway. Parked in the driveway of that corner house was a huge, polished black and chrome, Lincoln Continental. It was the most beautiful car I had ever seen. It was the biggest car I had ever seen. It was the shiniest car I had ever seen. And, I wanted to have one more than any car I had ever seen. To this young boy, that car was the pure and unquestionable definition of life success.

Most Sundays, I would simply admire the car quietly as the family drove by listening to the comments about what had occurred in church that morning and the length of the minister's sermon. While driving by one day, I just couldn't hold my admiration any longer. From my place in the backseat I popped up, "I wish we could have a car like that black Lincoln Continental." What I expected in reply was to just get a shrug from my parents or perhaps an admonition that to own that kind of car would be a waste. Maybe I would hear a by-and-by promise that someday if I worked hard, studied hard and kept my room clean (that always seemed to be the answer to everything) that I would be able to have a car just like that Lincoln.

You can imagine what shock and delight overwhelmed me when my father replied very matter-of-factly, "We can have one of those if you really want." I was elated! I could already see our family driving down Main Street to church in that car and all the people in town stopping to take a look at us. It would be fantastic. But, as quickly as that vision came to me, so did the question; "Why didn't we have one now then?"

My father was not one who would ever be looked upon as a philosopher. He was skilled at cutting to the chase and putting ideas about life and reality into very uncomplicated terms. When I asked him when and how we could get one, and if we really could have one, my father's answer was matter-of-fact and straight to the point. "I could go to Wichita and buy one of those tomorrow if that's what you really want." My young boy grin and excitement grew. "Of course," my father continued, "we will need to move into a smaller house. You will need to get by with fewer new clothes. You will need to give up sports so you'll have time to work too, and we won't be going on vacation. But it's no problem, we can have one."

You see, in my father's clear and descriptive way, he was simply reminding me that you can have virtually anything you want, if you're willing to pay the price. The question is, what was I willing to pay and to give up to get something else that I believed to be the most important thing in the world? He reminded me of an important question to be asked in life, "What will you surrender, in order to gain what you claim is most important?" The price of something is always determined by what you are willing to give. The price that is paid will always change a life.

I never did get one of those big black Lincolns to drive around town, but that's all right. Now all the kids wave at me when I ride by on my custom Harley...

I Am or Not

For much of my pre-teenage growing up years, my father was a smoker. Now to say he was a "smoker" is a bit of an understatement. He consumed the smoke of an average of two and one-half packs of cigarettes each day and in between cigarettes, he had a pipe in his mouth. When I was very young, I thought it was great to go to the corner grocery store with him. I got to go inside and buy his carton of cigarettes and with the change get a package of gum for me. I thought I was really grown up on the Fourth of July when I could smoke and use the hot end of the cigarette to light the fuse of my firecracker. As I got older, I had my times of sneaking around to secretly have a smoke with friends even though I knew it was wrong. When the government started putting written warnings on all the tobacco products it made no difference to me.

My dad also knew it wasn't good for him, and he tried several times to quit. But, as anyone who has a smoking history and has tried to quit knows, it feels like it is impossible to do. Over the years of his efforts to quit, he tried a long list of methods but could always come up with a reason the he had to start in again. Undoubtedly, the craziest excuse to light up again was when he suffered a collapsed lung during the time he was trying to quit. He told himself that it was the quitting that caused his medical problem. Usually his attempts at stopping were programs that let him slow down gradually.

One day he came home after work and I noticed that he wasn't smoking. When I questioned him, he announced that he had quit. . . again. He said that a co-worker at the Santa Fe Railroad Depot where he worked had come to work that morning, bragging about the fact that he had stopped smoking. A conversation between my dad and his co-worker became a friendly challenge and competition. My dad announced to his friend that "anyone could quit if they wanted to." The co-worker responded, "Well, I don't see you stopping!" My father then said that he needed to go to the store and buy more cigarettes, so he just wouldn't go. He claimed that he would quit for longer than his friend. The challenge was issued and accepted and both men started the contest that both assumed would only last a few days. My dad's co-worker began to smoke again within the week. My father never began again and spent the last ten years of his life, tobacco free.

My father discovered two things that made all the difference in his ability to do what he knew he should. He found a substitute in lemon drops. For the years following his quitting, he devoured bag after bag of the yellow drops. If I had invested in the company that produced the lemon drops, I would now be a rich man! The other discovery was really the more important of the two. I asked him why he didn't just taper off until he had quit. That would have been easier. He simply said, "Some things you don't do part-way. Either I quit or I didn't."

I sometimes hear people referring to a woman who is

expecting a child, nearing the delivery date, as being "really pregnant." Well, that's a little silly to say. You are or you are not. You cannot be "a little bit." There are some things that are like that from moment to moment – from decision to decision. I am on a diet, or I am not. I am truthful, or I am not. I am loving, or I am not. I am faithful, or I am not. This is not to say that I am any of these things, absolutely and once and for all. I have my moments of each, but in those moments – I am or I am not…

A Lady Named Delilah

I would bet that everyone of my general age – somewhere between 50 and 100 years old – who went to a Protestant church located in America's heartland knew someone like her. Every Sunday morning she sat at the front of the sanctuary for worship. Of course when I say "at the front" that means as close to the front as anyone gets in most churches, which is four rows back from the first pew in line. Her name was Delilah Spriggs. No, I did not make that up. That was her real name.

I think that once upon a time, she had been a schoolteacher, but that was not during my lifetime. I know that she taught one of the adult Sunday School classes that met during the hour before worship began because my father was a faithful attendee of her class. He never talked about what she taught but I know he liked whatever it was or however she did it because he got up early on Sunday mornings to get there. Every Sunday morning she sat in her owned pew with her lady friends that were born in some past century with her.

Actually, she could have positioned herself on any

pew and she would have been noticed. She was not a large lady by football standards but seemed larger than she was because of her Sunday morning wardrobe. She always wore a cotton dress with a bouquet of multi-colored flowers printed into the cloth. When she sat, the hem of the skirt covered her knees and almost made it down to meet the tops of nylon hose that were rolled down to just below where the skirt ended. The most attention getting of her ensemble though was her hat. Every Sunday a different view-blocking art piece topped the tight bun hairdo. It was never a small pillbox hat that would have made Jackie Kennedy proud or some small, feathered piece lying closely against her forehead. Her headpieces would extend from one of her shoulders, across to the other. On a few of her hats, the brim could have been used as a landing strip for a small plane. Rising up from the surface of the hat would be enough feathers to convince the congregation that somewhere in her family history, she had been a Cherokee chief. Sometimes, the feathers were still attached to a stuffed bird of some kind, perched like it had swooped down to recover some of the feathers that this woman had stolen.

Delilah was a teacher and whether she was a paid professional or of just her Sunday School class filled with my father and his friends, she had a "school teacher voice." It was a voice that demanded to be heard even when speaking outside of the classroom. And did I mention, Delilah Spriggs was not a shy person?

One Sunday morning, Delilah and her bird feather and flower hat sat in her pew with her lady friends and I sat with my family in our owned pew 4 or 5 rows behind her. I was old enough to know I was supposed to be quiet and pay attention but not old enough to always do what I knew. That morning, the preacher who had once been a college professor was explaining to us (again) every possible meaning of a word out of the Bible. Under his well-educated guidance, we explored every possible meaning of that Greek word in the holy text and even without a watch, I knew we were not getting out of church at a decent time.

At the twenty minute mark of the sermon, the preacher did not seem to be anywhere near a concluding point. As I wiggled just enough to get a look from my mother who was still barely awake, I heard it! From a voice hidden beneath that birds and feathers and flowers, a schoolteacher type voice, I heard, "My God...he's going to preach us into Tuesday!"

In the church, I was brought up to believe that the purpose of the sermon was to "preach us into heaven" or maybe even "into a closer relationship with God." That's not what she said.

Every Sunday morning when I look out from the pulpit, very little that I learned in seminary preaching class crosses my mind. However, I do search the pews and I can still hear the words of the wise little lady with a funny hat and a funnier name...

Recycled Jesus

In church language it is called "stewardship." Sometimes it is referred to as "responsible spending." For others, it is about "budget management." Whatever it is called, it is about how to spend the money that comes into the church in a way that makes God happy. Most of the time, it also means making the majority of the church board happy. The problem is that every church that I am aware of never has enough. The fact that that there is always more to do than there is money to pay for leads to some unique and funny happenings in the church.

If you ever take a site-seeing tour of a church facility you will find the classrooms furnished with every style of furniture that has been in the homes of members for the last twenty-five years. There must be something universal about the belief that furniture that is too worn or outdated for our home is exactly what the church needs. We will even deliver!

Sometimes, the minister spearheads the cost-cutting effort. I remember one minister friend who wanted to put an end to wasteful use of throwaway cups for the church members' Sunday morning coffee. Since he was taller than anyone else in the church, he began to hide the packages of cups in the drop ceiling of the church kitchen that only he could reach. He also decided that it would be a cost saving measure to turn off the air-conditioning units after each use and turn them on only a few minutes before they were needed. After the third compressor on the unit had to be replaced, he was convinced that he was not saving the church any money. The final attempt at "responsible spending" came when he discovered that a powdered artificial grape drink was the same color and similar taste as the grape juice used for weekly communion. That idea lasted a total of two weeks!

Weekly communion in the Christian Church and Churches of Christ is at the very heart of every worship service. The American history that gave birth to these protestant congregations was focused on the central importance of communion. In Christian Churches, the leadership can tinker with almost anything except the communion. Every Sunday I heard a reminder that the little piece of hard bread is Jesus' body and the grape juice in the little cup is Jesus' blood. This was Jesus that became a part of me. But since we have it every week, it does have a cost. Since everyone present in worship is invited to participate it is important that enough is prepared so no one is left out. The only way to make sure there are enough little glass or plastic cups filled and available is to prepare more than the average weekly attendance. The only way to be absolutely sure there will be enough is to prepare for an Easter-size crowd every week. However, this does mean that on every Sunday there are many full cups left unused. This was a fact that did not go unnoticed by two of the ladies that were in charge of preparing the communion in the church where I grew up.

The two ladies, who were trained about "responsible spending" in the school of the Great Depression, decided it was their Christian responsibility to do something about the weekly waste. They began pouring the leftover grape juice from each little communion shot glass back into the bottle of juice kept in the church refrigerator but left out on the kitchen counter during the Sunday morning worship.

Nothing looked or tasted any different after the first Sunday of recycled juice. After the second week, a few extra bubbles could be seen floating at the top of each filled communion cup. On the third week, I would have sworn that there was a slight tinge of pink around the edge of the juice where it nestled against the inside of the cup. On the fourth Sunday morning, when it was time for the trays to be passed that held the cups of recycled juice, representing the blood of Jesus, there just a hint of unusual odor that drifted through the sanctuary. As the trays were passed along each pew, the expressions on the faces of each worshipper, changed sip after sip. Eyes squinted, lips tightened together, expressions of wonder and question were shared back and forth and there were a few choking sounds as the now fermented communion made its way into the body and soul. When the tray reached me, I tossed back the communion in one gulp like a cowboy leaning against the saloon bar in a western movie. I should have been upset but I thought it was great. It was the closest thing to real wine I had ever tasted! As I glanced over at an old Elder sitting across the aisle, I would have sworn that he had the beginnings of smile on his face too.

After the "almost wine" episode, the church leaders decided that we could cut the church budget other places so we could have fresh grape juice each week for communion.

Over the years, at youth led worship services, church camps and in an airport in South America, I have celebrated the communion using juice, water, fruit punch, strawberry cola and yes, even real wine. Each time, in every liquid used to represent the life and love of Jesus, the moment has been special. It has never been about what filled the cup...

Only One?

Maybe I'm getting a head start on "Christmas thinking" here, but I might as well join the crowd of shopping centers, discount superstores and television advertisements.

In my immediate and extended family, the concepts of Christmas and gift were always bound together. One always created an expectation of the other. In fact, we had a family tradition that I have only observed with my relatives.

On Christmas morning, sometimes before dawn, the phone would ring and in a voice that often was only half awake, it would be answered. But the Christmas morning greeting was never a "hello" or "good morning" or even "Merry Christmas!" It was of ultimate importance that the first words out of the receiver were "Christmas Gift!"

According to family legend the person who said those magical words first was entitled to a present from the one who was slower to respond. And so it went, every Christmas morning, either by phone or in person, a contest to get presents. Of course, everyone still got the presents that had been planned and purchased weeks earlier, but it was a fun contest nonetheless. According to the history of the practice that I learned after I was well into adulthood, it began back in the days of slavery. Christmas day was the only day that was not a day of work and the slaves were allowed to come to the owner's back door and after knocking they would try to say "Christmas gift" to the owner. If the slave said it first they would receive a small gift of meat or sweets, but if too slow, they walked away empty-handed.

In our modern family tradition, it was just a game to be played. Sometimes though, the game would lead to embarrassing results when following a screaming "Christmas gift" was delivered over the telephone, the response was from a neighbor who had called to say that her brother had been killed the night before.

I can remember another Christmas that was all about gifts too. On that Christmas morning, package unwrapping started out as disappointment.

The days leading up to Christmas day often involved a great degree of detective work. I had spent days before Christmas sorting through the packages beneath the tree, only finding one with my name on it. Imagine that! Only ONE! Of course my birthday had been just a couple weeks earlier and had been a pretty profitable day, but now this was Christmas. That's a different day altogether! Each day I would un-stack and look and check labels and each day there was just one box for me. It was a large sized box, but it was only one.

As the mornings counted down toward Christmas, the disappointment and frustration only grew. And, as the great morning approached, frustration began to turn into bitterness. Everyone else in the family had more than one package and each one had a package from me. It was unfair and I suspect my grumpy expression as Christmas morning dawned proclaimed that unfairness to the world. With only one package to tear into, I was in no hurry to get it over with and then have to sit and watch everyone else who was being treated so much better.

Finally, after everyone had opened at least one package and with a bright smile on her face, my mother pulled my one package across the wooden floor until it sat in front of me. Only one package! Her smile and that of my Dad seemed to grow brighter and larger as I began to slowly pull the Christmas wrapping back and yanked the taped lid of the box open. The open cardboard flaps revealed more wrapping paper that hid other boxes. Pulling them out, one by one, I counted. One, two, three . . . another and another . . . some small, some larger . . . each one just inviting me to tear in and discover what wonders lay inside. Inside the one present were ten gifts, each one to be enjoyed, played with, worn or eaten. I was too busy to look, but I suspect the only joy greater than mine was displayed on the faces of parents who had given them to me. There was only one box, but many gifts.

Jesus told a parable which has become familiar to many people. It's a story about a wealthy man who gave his servants gifts with the instruction that the servants do something with what he had given them. To one person he gave one gift, to another he gave five gifts and to one he gave ten gifts. I remember the unique way that Jesus told it and how the story turned out. The story told about the pleasure of the man when the receivers of the five and ten gifts had doubled what they were given by using each of the gifts. The story does not end so well for the one gift person who was afraid to take any chances or making any mistakes. He just dug a hole and buried what he had.

I read that story and usually glumly put myself in the place of the one-gift servant. I can do a little, but after all, not much. But then I recall that Christmas morning a long time ago and guess what? I am not a one-gift person! I'm pretty sure that no one I know is. I am not even a five-gift servant. I am with the ten-gift folks. With voice, arms, hands, legs, ears, eyes, homes, families, friends, food, church, faith, hope, love and really the list goes well past ten. There is no end to what I can do.

Christmas Gift…

Running the Lake

There are a few poor choices you can get away with and there are quite a few that you cannot. If you grow up in a small town, the list of things that you cannot get away with grows even longer. It is a lesson learned best at a young age but you are never too old to learn. It is especially true when the lesson concerns adventures in the automobile.

On the northern outskirts of the little county seat town that was the place of my growing up was the Barber County Lake. The lake was not quite big enough for large motorboats, but it was just right for fishing, picnics and getting into trouble. Beginning at the dam that formed the south boundary, roads of dirt and loose rock almost encircled the lake on both sides. In most places those vehicle paths that were called roads were just wide enough for one car and to meet another meant that someone had to steer into the uncut weeds that lined the dirt. Because the lake was not a great winter vacation destination, there was very little traffic on the lake roads during the school year. That made it a perfect place to learn to drive and to perfect driving skills. It was practicing those other driving skills that got me into trouble.

For a few high school age boys, there was an activity

that was generally referred to as "running the lake." It was not an activity that involved putting on jogging shoes and getting exercise on foot. The fun was created by driving your car along those narrow dirt roads from the dam on the south to the circle that was the conclusion of the road at the north end and returning to the starting point. The intent was to travel that hometown raceway in as little elapsed time as possible. And, I was good!

Even though I drove a 1951 Chevrolet 4-door sedan with a six-cylinder engine and two-speed "slush-box" automatic transmission with a low gear that did not work, I held the fastest time for making that run. There was a challenging excitement to the feel of tires slipping on loose dirt and rocks flying into the grass, as the old faded green and gray car slid sideways around hairpin curves. It took steel nerves and the reflexes of a bootlegger to negotiate running the lake at full speed. The one local police officer would occasionally deliver a hard stare to me as I came out of the gate of the lake property and onto the paved city street, but I never was stopped or caught, at least not officially.

One Sunday afternoon, just before heading home for supper, I finished one of the fastest runs of my racing career. After running the lake in record time, I popped out onto the city street and saw no one around. I knew I had chalked up another near perfect run that would be remembered in the stories of local folklore. When I parked along the curb in front of my house, I was just a little surprised to see my father sitting on the front step of the house with a cup of steaming instant coffee in his hand. Still patting myself on the back for my driving success I did not notice the expression on my father's face until I was almost to the front door. When I finally looked, I was met with rigidly set lips and a darkened stare that made me wonder who had died. His first words let me know that the life about to be ended was mine. What he said was, "We just got a telephone call about you." There really was nothing more that needed to be said, but he continued, "They wanted us to know about your driving around the lake." I was caught with no defense and no escape and no words except, "who called?" That question has never been answered. I mumbled something about being sorry and that it would never happen again, and so began one of the most miserable weeks of my young life.

That telephone call came to my parents one week before the annual high school prom. The prom was a once a year event that I had planned to attend with a female classmate. It was a night that I had planned to drive the two-year old family Oldsmobile instead of my sixteen-year old Chevrolet. My old car was perfect for running the lake but not for impressing a date. With that one telephone call, my vision of a wonderful evening quickly faded.

I was left with a dilemma and a decision. I wondered if I should save the embarrassment of an old car and make up a reason to cancel my prom plans? Should I explain the situation to my date and let her decide to change her mind? Should I try to arrange a last minute sharing of rides with a friend and his date? I despised the anonymous caller but also my poor choices that led me to disappoint my parents, their friends, my friends and myself. I decided to warn my prom date and give her the chance to change her choice of evening attire or evening partner. Much to my surprise, her decision was to not make any change at all.

As the miserable week made its way toward Saturday evening, I do not remember speaking more than five or six sentences to my father. I knew that I had disappointed him beyond conversation. As Saturday afternoon turned into evening, I reluctantly put on my best suit, dress shirt and tie and presented my dressed-up self to my parents before heading toward the old car sitting at the curb.

My father was a man who believed greatly in personal responsibility, justice and paying your debts. He was a man who believed deeply in family reputation in a small town where everyone knew everyone. My father was a man who never overlooked the mistakes of his children, but he did look beyond those mistakes. I knew all of that about my father, but I did not know that he knew me so well.

As I made my way to our front door, my father placed his hand on my back and dropped the keys of the family Oldsmobile into my hands. As I looked at him in disbelief, all he said was, "Be careful, I love you." I was because I knew he did …

Fired

No question about it, I should have been fired. It was not a career. It was a high school job but it provided gas money, drive-in money and a little bit of teenage independence. My job was better than some of my friends who had to work in the heat on the farm. The grocery store had air-conditioning and regular hours. The regular hours are what got me into trouble.

Mr. Howard owned the grocery store that had his name on a large red and white sign over the street. Our families had known each other for years. We went to the same church. His daughter was a classmate of my sister. It was the only place we ever bought groceries. Mr. Howard was a well-respected man but he had expectations of the people on his payroll and that included a 17 year old who bagged groceries, stocked shelves and cleaned floors. Expectations and a life long commitment to hard work made Mr. Howard a very successful businessman. Those expectations included arriving on time, not leaving before time, doing your work the best you could in between and never let a customer see you standing around not doing something. I usually did my job according to those requirements, but then love happened.

Looking back, I know it wasn't what I know now as love, but it was feeling pretty much like it at the time. It was a new feeling so I was without any comparisons. That makes first times on anything the most exciting but also the most difficult. The beautiful blonde had moved to town for one year and we had dated with a fair amount of regularity. But, after a short school year and part of the summer, she had moved back to her previous home 30 miles away. We kept in touch by phone for a while and even saw each other a couple of times. Then, it ended. It was a story that many could tell, but for me, it was a first.

One morning, in the middle of shelves to be refilled and groceries to be carried out for customers I looked up to see her walking down the bread aisle straight toward me. She was not alone. Next to her walked a man, not another teenage boy, but someone older, taller and broader than me. He must have been at least twenty years old! Together, the three of us went outside the back door and there it was explained to me in exacting detail, that I was no longer in the romantic picture. I was left with no doubt about the sincerity of her message.

I was heartbroken, confused, angry, frustrated, alone and embarrassed all at the same time. There was much that I did not know at that moment but I did know that I did not want to be there. I did not want to see anyone or talk to anyone and I certainly did not want to carry any groceries. I could not have cared any less about my job or Mr. Howard's expectations. So, I left. I did not tell anyone that I was taking my fifteen-minute coffee break early and I did not tell anyone what had happened. I climbed into my car and drove away. I drove all around town several times. I drove to the county lake and sat in my car listening to song after song on the radio. My coffee break grew into lunchtime and lunch into the beginning of the afternoon. By the time I walked into the back door of my job, I had been gone for over three hours. I had taken a huge piece out of my workday and cut the heart out of what was expected of me.

As I walked back into the store and tied my white apron around my waist, I knew I was going to be fired. I deserved to be fired. The other employees had missed some of their deserved time out of the store because they had to fill in for me. They had every right to be angry even though no one said a word as I walked past them toward the front and Mr. Howard's office. If I had been my co-worker, I would have been angry. If I were my boss, I would have escorted me to the door.

Mr. Howard was out of the store when I got to the front, so I found an empty aisle and began to stack vegetable cans on the shelves. After five minutes that felt like forever, I could see the moment I deserved but dreaded walking toward me. As I stood before the man I had disappointed so much, I began to untie my apron in preparation for what I knew was about to happen. I began to see the faces of my parents as I explained that I had been fired. Face to face with Mr. Howard, I heard him say, "Coffee breaks in this store are fifteen minutes. Remember that." He then turned and walked back to his office.

I do not know if someone had told him what happened. I do not know if he had seen and heard part of the conversation I experienced that morning. I do not know if he could see the hurt on my face. I do not know if he had remembered a time that he felt like me. So many things I do not know about that day and Mr. Howard. What I do know is that I deserved to lose and instead I received. I think I received a gift called grace...

Pick Just One?

Some of the most respected and dedicated men I have known were elders in the Christian Church of my growing-up years. I have to say men because in the traditional belief of that church, only men could be church leaders. It was a time before some of us began to realize that God chose leaders based on gifts rather than gender. But even though the group was limited to males only, that did not change the way I admired what I observed in their lives. If I was given the task of selecting the one most deserving to receive special recognition, I am not sure who would have been my choice.

One of the elders was a man who was very successful in his own business. He did not flaunt his wealth but everyone in the county knew he had plenty. His family attended the church and his children were sometimes active in Sunday school classes and evening youth activities. He came to church on a regular basis, which is to say at least once a month. He was a generous man with his financial support of the church and sometimes even gave extra when the need arose. There were a few times at the end of the month that bills would have been left unpaid if not for his generous contribution. As far as I am aware, he never made a big show of his giving and never expected any special attention in return. He took account of what he had and generously shared for the good of the church.

A second man included in this group of elders had a middle class job with a middle class income. He was a regular contributor to the church, giving a percentage of his take home salary. However, the amount that he contributed to the financial needs of the church was no comparison to the business owner. This man also had a family that was active in the programs of the church. His wife helped in teaching and the work allowed to be done by the women. The man's children were active in classes and also in the weekly youth activities. This elder did not work with extra programs in the church but was very active with the children of the community. He was a community leader in Boy Scouts and coached summer league baseball for many years. At his funeral, the pews were filled with young men who had been influenced by his work throughout the city. He never went door-to-door inviting people to come to church but there were families who came because of his casual invitation to neighbors and co-workers.

The third elder was completely unlike the other two in many ways. This man never married and so he had no wife or children to bring to church. He and his brothers operated a farm outside of town and rumors ran through town conversation about his "secret wealth." Knowing the man for many years, I did not believe any of the stories. This elder was present every time the church doors were open. He did not have biological children of his own but he cared about and was a friend to every child that grew up as a part of that church. Every Sunday evening when meetings for the high school youth were over, he would take everyone who wanted to go to the local bowling lanes. He would pay for every pair of rented bowling shoes and every game played. If we wanted a coke to drink, he would buy it and include a package of salted peanuts to pour into the bottle. Every young person in that church that graduated from high school got a card and a small graduation present. Through my first years of college, I wore the watch that I received from him. In fact, there was one young man in the church that this elder tried to talk into becoming a minister. The man even offered to pay his way through school if the graduating student would choose that life path. It was an offer never accepted, but sincerely made none-the-less.

Three elders served in a congregation in such different ways. If I were to choose the most important, who would it be? If I had to decide which one of these three did the most for God, would it be the first, the second or the third?

Yes...

Who Cares?

Sometimes the dream was to be a major league baseball player. Sometimes that dream changed into visions of sitting in the White House as President of the United States. Once in a while when science classes did not seem too hard, a doctor performing heart surgery seemed like a great choice. But, truth be told, my dream that never changed was to be a rock-and-roll star. Taking my place on stage in front of thousands of screaming fans, mostly female, was a dream that started in third grade, and I'm not sure that it has completely faded yet.

That dream of musical screaming stardom took me to the neighbor's garage for parties with classmates. We would celebrate for almost any reason; from birthdays to end-beginning-middle of school. As records played (yes it was that long ago), something could always be found to serve as an impromptu stage. The chair or box or wagon became the place for sharing the latest chart topper.

I suppose it was an appreciation for a son's dream that would lead my father to purchase for his son a gold, metal-flake electric guitar that would play music the father didn't like at a volume that he liked even less.

It was that dream that led me, with guitar in hand, to sneak into my hometown church and meet the minister's son. Together and sometimes joined by another friend, the three of us would switch on the sanctuary pipe organ and play music that would send the church elders to their knees in prayer for our trio of souls.

But, dreams while perhaps not surrendered, can take on different colors and shapes after a while. Sometimes a golden instrument, amplified sound and stardom are replaced by a brown acoustic guitar with more gentle strings. The adoring fans become friends and family in rows of pews; the stage becomes a chancel and songs about lovers become songs about love.

On Sunday morning, with guitar in hand, I stood in the church of my new hometown. I didn't even have to sneak in. I had been invited to play and sing by those people who I deeply respected, sitting in the pews. I had chosen and practiced a song familiar to them all. It was a song I had heard and sometimes even sung since I was a young boy.

As the congregation waited, I placed the open hymnbook on the music stand and began to move my fingers across the guitar strings. As the words of the old song came to mind, I passed them on to the crowd. The first verse went smoothly but as I brought the refrain to an end to start up the pathway of the next verse, nerves grabbed my hands, my memory and my voice. The following moments of struggle to find the right words and finish the song lasted what seemed for hours. When the song came to a merciful end, the guitar was almost tossed into its case while the strings still vibrated. Embarrassed, ashamed, alone and angry I tried to sneak to the back of the room where I could not be seen.

It was my intention as the now dreamless entertainer, to escape the building and its occupants as soon as the final amen had been said. I almost made it! But standing in the way, blocking my escape was Herb.

Herb was an elder of the congregation. In fact both Herb and his wife helped found the congregation, and both served as leaders. Herb was more than the holder of a church title. With his kind ways, he had helped teach all of us how to hug and find a minute of joy in every day. There was no path around Herb.

Just a little bit of a grin underlined an expression of questioning when Herb spoke. He said, almost apologetically, "I really liked the song, but I think I missed part of it. I forget, what was that middle part of the second verse?"

Those lost words of the old hymn, now found, ask. "If I falter Lord, who cares?"

Herb smiled, winked and stepped aside to make a path…

Jake's Gift

"God doesn't give us more than we can handle." That is a nice thought. Hanging onto that idea might give us confidence to wade through seemingly tough times. The trouble is that it's not true. As much as we quote it like scripture, it's nowhere to be found. And, what does it say about God? Doesn't that belief make the Creator some heavenly tyrant who piles burdens on us just to see how much we can take? Without God adding more, there are plenty enough burdens that break our hearts, our spirits and even our wills to go on.

Standing at the miniature casket, where the child of a friend now lies surrounded by his favorite stuffed toys and coloring books, is not a moment of God's testing. As the sky blue metal lid closes over dreams and hopes, God is not penciling in our grade because of our ability to handle the tears.

Airliners flying into skyscrapers, fathers taking their own lives, children abused and the helpless poor sitting in the rain while bellies grow silent in spite of emptiness cannot be the intention of a Giver of every good and perfect gift.

While God may not give us safe passage around the spirit smashing events of life, God does give us something even better. God does not give a grade so much as a gift. We are given companions for the journey. We are given one another.

An old wise man once reminds us that what one cannot lift, two can carry. And, the companions that travel with us best, whose words comfort us most and whose acts of kindness touch us most deeply are not those few souls that seem to skip through life smiling without a care in the world. The companion whose presence and embrace are most healing is the one whose face shows the lines of life lived and weathered. It is the one who walks beside us and whose walk is slightly bent over from the weight of heartbreak.

My father died unexpectedly at the age of 53. When the moment came, I was a grown-up, twenty-two years old. There are some things that I remember with unclouded clarity of those days of preparation for and the service of celebrating his life. I can recall those church friends of the family who brought over plates of food, but I can't tell you what the dishes were. I cannot remember the names of the songs sung but I remember the faces of those who sang. I cannot tell you a single word that the minister of the church, a close friend of my father's, spoke but I will never forget the constant smile on his face that caught his tears.

All of those memories are overwhelmed by what happened to me as the service at the church ended. As I walked down the center aisle with my mother tightly gripping one arm and surrounded by the rest of the family, I almost stopped in my escape. Looking up for a moment, I saw the face of Jake. His warm eyes were following me as we slowly followed the casket. I could not believe that he was there.

Jake was a college friend with whom I shared a love of football, our social-service club and golf outings in place of going to class on warm spring days. I had not seen or talked to Jake for almost a year since our graduation. He lived in southern Oklahoma while I lived in northern Kansas. How did he know?

After the casket had been placed in the hearse for its journey to a family burial plot, I searched the crowd standing on the church lawn for any sign of Jake. He knew no one else in the crowd so as he stood alone I was able to find him. As we met, there were no words said except perhaps a stuttering thank-you from me and a hug from him.

As I returned to the family car, that moment of loss became also a moment of joy. Jake was there for me. Jake was there because he knew. Jake knew because he had held his mother's arm as they followed the casket of his father down the center aisle of their family church years before. Jake was a gift.

I am not just one who receives God's gift of companions for my journey I am God's gift into the journey of another. It is a gift that says I don't have all the answers to give you, but I have walked a similar road.

God also gives us another gift – another companion – God's own self.

A follower of Jesus named Paul once listed all the really big burdens of life. It was a list that did not include a hangnail or bad hair day, no two penny rise in gas prices or loss by a favorite football team. In the middle of all that, there is a promise that we will never have to face those times alone.

Sometimes the companionship of God comes in a face and voice easy to recognize because we encounter it across the dinner table, in the workplace or classroom, in a senior citizen center or daycare. Sometimes it comes as a whisper of comfort without words and an embrace of compassion from a presence we may not see but we know as surely as we know the sun and moon and stars that give light in the darkest night. Sometimes it comes at the close of a tearstained prayer. Sometimes it is heard in the pause when we struggle to find the next words and sometimes even before we begin to utter our first cry for help.

These gifts transform the moment because they change us. God does not wrap us up in some spiritual plastic wrap, shutting us off, insulating us from all the ups and downs of life. We can't be insulated from the burden of pain without also surrendering the celebration of joy. Insulation in our houses keeps out the cold and warmth alike.

With both hands of love I reach out to receive and to give. I stand a little straighter and so does someone else. My steps are a little steadier and so are those who walk beside me. There is joy in the journey for me and those whose lives reach out to me and whose lives I reach out and touch.

I learned that from Jake…

Uninvited

He was the reason I was there, which made him the recipient of my stumbling attempt. This was not the first time I had visited someone in the hospital. It was not even the first time I had visited someone who was not a member of the family. Some of the people that I had visited had been members of the same church that I had attended and my visit was on behalf of that church. But those visits had been before I began seminary to become a minister. Those earlier visits were before I was expected to know what I was doing. So when a non-active member of my student church in Texas became a patient in a Dallas Hospital, I was not quite sure what I should say to him.

I had received a telephone call from Carl's family that he had been diagnosed with lung cancer and they would appreciate it if I would stop in to see him. I wondered what they expected me to say to a man who I had never met, who didn't come to the church and who was chewing on what the doctors had told him. Standing next to his bed, I introduced myself as the minister of his wife and son's church. The look that reflected back to me said, "O my God, they've sent the priest to give me last rites!" I mumbled something about just wanting to let him know that he was in our prayers and I would be available to him any time he wanted. I offered to say a prayer over him and I suspect it was only out of Southern politeness that he let me hold his hand and say a very short prayer. That was the beginning, but that was not the end of visits between Carl and me.

Over the following several weeks, Carl and I had several visits. Sometimes we were at the hospital and sometimes at his house. His physical condition sometimes improved between visits and sometimes a new complication was discovered. He saw no need for a long routine of treatments and his family lovingly allowed him that choice with little argument. Sometimes we would have a prayer together before I left and sometimes we just talked. There is something holy about a grandfather who can hang up his rough exterior overcoat and talk with pride and love about his grandchildren and their parents.

It only happened a couple of times but Carl even made it to church during those months that our friendship grew. When his body would be slapped with another problem the church would remember him in prayer. On one or two occasions, an old fishing buddy, neighbor or business acquaintance would drop by for a short visit and a few laughs in the middle of retold stories. He and I had a pretty big pile of funny stories and shared laughs, too. I think sometimes, if people could hear our laughing they would think that we really did not know how serious his condition was. If they looked at another time as the cancer moved from his lungs into the bones of his legs and back, they would know that he and I knew all too well. We came to know that if you give yourself permission to cry you also give yourself permission to laugh. The breath that creates both the laugh and the cry come from the same place and tears can roll in the midst of either sound.

As Carl's life approached its final experiences, he went to live in a skilled nursing facility where he could receive the drugs needed to ease the pain that filled his bones. It was one afternoon, in that place of anticipated death that uncontrolled laughter could be heard. In fact, the laughter seemed so out of place for some nurses who heard that they came running into the room fearing the worse and left totally confused.

Carl and I were having one of our broad topic conversations when the subject of heaven and hell was touched upon. I am not positive, but I am pretty sure that he is the one that added it to our conversation. Our discussion began with a serious discussion about God's grace and about forgiveness for whatever our life may have been. We talked about a God we had talked about on other occasions. We retold stories about a prodigal son and a woman at a well and few other favorites. Then Carl began to smile and I began to pat myself on the back for helping him find peace in the pain. He then grinned and stated with absolute certainty that he was going to heaven because there was no way the devil would let him into hell. As he spoke I began to laugh too because I knew what he was saying. You see, Carl had spent his life in business as the owner of a successful air-conditioning company. In the early days of the company he was both salesman and installer. In the same moment, we both had the image of Carl being turned away at the gates of hell because no devil in his right mind would let an air-conditioning installer in.

We laughed at the image and laughed in the pain and laughed in our confidence in God and laughed in our love for one another and laughed in the memories that would make me laugh even today.

In those moments, a laughter that echoed through the halls and brought nurses running to see what all the noise was about was not really about something silly but was the sound of joy shared. The sound of the laughter echoed through the moment and through the church a few days later as I said goodbye to my friend. In the sound of joy, there was Carl's voice and my voice and the voice of Another...

A Brother's Hug

A lot sure can change in a short six years. Some changes are just a natural progression of age like less hair and what is left turns gray. I swear I can do all the things I did when I was younger but not as fast or for as long and it takes me much more time to recover. Those are changes I may not like but there is little I can do about them. But there are also those changes in thought, perception and belief that are all of my choosing. Those changes may seem easier to make, but they really are the difficult ones.

    Six years had passed since I graduated from undergraduate school in Oklahoma. My leaving college was just a little before Richard Nixon left the White House. During those six years I had become a father of two sons and worked as a police detective in a suburb of the Kansas City metropolitan area. During that time I found myself no longer able to talk myself out of responding to what I believed to be an unrelenting nudge to change life plans and prepare for professional ministry. So, on a frigid and icy day in January, the whole family began a trek that would first stop for three and one half years at seminary in Ft. Worth, Texas.

    I discovered that while I had been out of the

classroom, I was not the only thing that had changed. The first writing assignment in a class on church history was returned looking more bloodied than people I had previously pulled out of mangled automobiles. Every page of my attempt at written clarity had been marked with bright red lines and circles. No one had told me that gender specific language was no longer acceptable. During the years earlier there had been no problem with references such as "Man and Mankind." Back then, everyone knew that God was "He" and "Father" was always correct. I was fortunate that the professor had a close acquaintance with grace and took the time to explain to me that God should be seen in broader and less limiting ways and my language should reflect that truth. But language was not the only change that I was to discover.

My second term at the seminary included taking a class on Church and Society. Looking only at the title, I thought to myself, "Just how hard can this be?" The classroom work progressed smoothly since I had opened up my language to a broader notion of God. Then came an invitation that reflected a different sort of change. The professor invited any students of all the classes to his home the next evening for conversations with a minister who had just publicly "come out" regarding his sexual orientation. I was all too familiar with the names given to his announced lifestyle. I had heard them all in my high school locker-room and on the streets where I had worked. I had been too uncomfortable with the slurs and name calling to join in but never uncomfortable enough to say something in defense of those who did not fit my "normal." As I looked down the information page the professor had distributed I saw the name of the minister who was to be there. A minister with that name and I had been undergraduate classmates just two years apart. We were not only classmates but also club brothers as members of the same social-service club at the university. He and I were different in many ways. I played all sports and he played none. He was a terrific student and I was less dedicated to my studies. I was in pretty good physical condition and he was obviously overweight. He was selected as the male student who most represented the highest standards of the university and I was hardly known outside of a small group of close friends. I could not imagine it was him and yet I knew that it was.

Hesitantly, I went to the professor's home the next night, hoping that I would see a stranger there and not a club brother. As I entered the front door I could hear a voice I recognized from the dorm hallways a lifetime of changes earlier. He smiled as he saw me enter and it was a smile of welcome that was much more at peace than the one I returned. My mind whirled with all kinds of questions. What should I say? What should I do? The typical way that he and I would greet another club brother in any other setting would be with a hug. Should I hug him now with what I knew? Would he accept the hug as a sign of brotherhood or would he read something romantic or sexual into it? If those new acquaintances saw us hug, what would they think? Would they suddenly have a new perception of me? I did not know. What I did know is that my lifelong presumptions about Gay and Straight and God were being questioned and were changing in those few short steps that separated me from my club brother.

Years later, long after that short walk, I heard another

person of great faith giving answer to the earliest question of humanity, "Am I my brother's keeper?" His answer is the one I heard whispered in a hug, "I am not my brother's keeper – I am my brother's brother..."

Go Where She Goes

She just showed up one Sunday morning. Looking a little lost, she was a mother who gripped the hand of an unwilling child in each of her weathered hands. Her little daughter appeared to be about six years old. Her hair was in brown curls that just tickled her shoulders. Velvet brown eyes scanned what seemed to the girl to be an oddly decorated room beginning to fill with people she had never seen before. The younger brother, who was about four years old, tried to dig his heals into the carpet and halt his mother's journey. A look of determination on the mother's face witnessed to her decision to bring herself and her children to the church she only knew from the outside.

 The family circle which contained the determined, the frightened and the unwilling found an almost empty pew toward the back and on the opposite side of the pulpit. Unfolding the printed-paper she was handed when they walked in, she began to explore a songbook taken out of the holder on the back of the pew in front of her. She located the songs that had the numbers corresponding to those printed on the paper and tried to remember any tunes from her childhood.

As the daughter continued to look at all the new sights to be found in the large room with the highest ceiling she had ever seen, her brother found the miniature truck he had stuffed into his pants pocket. He decided not to make his truck sounds as he traveled the highway along the back of the pew.

All the normal things happened that morning in worship. Everything went according to the printed plan that everyone had been handed but knew by repetition. Songs were sung, requests were prayed, a snack of grape juice and bread pieces was served, money was collected and I spoke for the regular allotted time.

I noticed the unnamed woman and sometimes interested children while I scanned the crowd that morning. I mentally thumbed through memory files trying to make a name and face connection just in case she was someone I should have known. No connection came, so when the service ended as quickly as possible, I made way to her. I stood and waited my turn to welcome and question her. I had to wait because Sue was talking to her.

I am completely convinced that every church needs to have someone like Sue. She was the closest thing we had in that congregation to a Protestant saint. Sue was not the kind of person that doused everyone she met with a syrupy spirituality. Her conversation was not punctuated with "praise Jesus" and "thank you Lord" in alternating sentences. It is just that she had faith that felt "real."

Looking from the outside, it appeared that faith would be easy for Sue because she seemed to have life easy. She lived in the big house just outside of town, her adult children were healthy and were successful and she had people around her much of the time. But, sometimes looking does not tell the whole story. Sue had grown up in a very male dominated place and time, which was hard for someone as smart and creative as she was. Her husband died after a heartbreaking struggle with cancer. She was one of the first women elders in the congregation and that was not always met with everyone's approval. On occasion, Sue was seen keeping company with people that were not the good church-going types.

After I had waited my turn, I welcomed the unknown woman, spoke to her children trying to make their escape out the front door and introduced myself. She replied with a first name and then volunteered her story.

The woman was going through the pain and fear of a divorce initiated by her husband. She went to a local attorney who had a good reputation to get advice about her situation. She said that as she sat in the attorney's office, she had never felt so alone and worthless. While she was waiting, an older lady at the receptionist desk began to talk to her. The woman discovered that the receptionist was actually the attorney's mother who was filling in during the real receptionist's vacation. As they talked about life and children and hope of a new beginning the woman's fear and loneliness began to fade. The substitute receptionist assured the woman that her son would be able to help her, but more than that, there was a God that still loved her and always would. She said that she was reminded of that every time she went to church. When the time for her legal consultation to begin the woman hesitated before going into the office, turned and asked the receptionist where she went to church. With a smile, she was given the

73

name and location.

As she finished her story, the woman looked at me and said, "I just knew I wanted to go where Sue goes…"

How To Move the Ball

There is an old saying in sports that goes something like: "Those who can, do and those who cannot, coach." After wearing my high school football uniform and watching from the bench for four years, I would say that I was prepared. With three sons who all loved sports and played every one invented, I would say that I had the opportunity. So when fifth grade football season arrived and another father was needed to coach a local youth league team, I was ready.

The father of the team quarterback would be the head coach, another father served as coach of the defense, and I had the glory position as coach of the offense. As the season began, I had visions of daily offers arriving by phone and mail for me to take over coaching duties at Oklahoma, Alabama or Notre Dame. Then, came the first practice.

In this mix of fifth grade, there were some who had played football since they could walk and some who were there only to live out the past dreams of other bench-sitting parents. We had running backs as fast as a hiccup and linemen as large as college freshmen. The defense was bloodthirsty and the offense learned plays that flowed like warm syrup over breakfast pancakes.

On the Saturday morning of the first game, the team pulled their black jerseys over shoulder-pads, mothers made sure that the laces on cleated shoes were double knotted and video cameras were focused on each star athlete. Then it began.

On our first chance to move the ball toward the goal line it looked like every moment of practice and great coaching had been lost. As the ball was hiked to our quarterback, every player on the line simply stood up, took one step backward and watched the player from the opposing team run past them and pile on top of our player holding the ball. Play after play, the same thing happened. During every timeout, the team was reminded, encouraged, threatened and bribed to block the defensive player in front of them. And, every play, the team moved further and further backwards. It was nothing less than an act of God's mercy that came to our rescue. The football league rules were that after one team got behind by so large of a score the scoreboard clock would not stop for any reason. With the game over, the team enjoyed their drinks and cookies and reminded themselves that it was only one game.

During the practices the next week, fundamentals were reviewed and practiced until the team was ready for the next Saturday contest. When Saturday morning arrived, jerseys were pulled on, laces were double-tied, cameras were focused and the adventure began and continued exactly like it had the week before. The ball was hiked, the players on the offensive line stood up, defensive players from the other team ran by and jumped on whoever was holding the ball.

Week after week the results were the same. Every practice, the skills were taught and encouragement given. I even tried some visual reminders. I bought black wristbands for every player and on the band I painted a large white arrow to serve as a reminder. The idea was that a player would see the arrow pointing forward in that last second before the play would begin and remember what to do and which direction to move. I got my first clue in futility when I noticed that on Saturday morning, many of the players had their wristbands on backwards!

By the time the season was two-thirds over we had scored no touchdowns. We had made only one first down. We had lost every game by huge margins and coaches were being threatened in late night phone calls. Parental disappointment was so deep that not a single video camera could be seen on Saturday morning. In desperation, I finally did the last thing I could think of- I called someone who knew what he was doing when it came to coaching football.

It had been years since I had seen or even talked to a friend from college who had become a very successful high school football coach in Colorado. But I was without answers or ideas. It turned out to be a call well worth the time and cost. After a few minutes of catching up on family news, I explained the real reason for my call and our team's inability to move the football. My friend listened quietly, but I could imagine the grin on his face and the laughing he was holding inside. After I had finished a very long description of the problem and a list of my failed solutions, he said that he had once coached a team with the same problem and had a suggestion for me to try. He said that the problem for young and inexperienced players is they feel isolated and are afraid of messing up, so they stand

and do nothing. He offered a suggestion of things for them to do. First, when the offensive players line up in position, have them be so close to one another that their feet and elbows touch. Second, when the ball is hiked, all the linemen should stay on their hands and toes, crawling forward together until they make contact with the other team's player in front of them. Finally, when they are in contact with the person in front of them, stand up and lift them up too. He said it would look ugly, but it would work.

Armed with his game plan, I arrived at that week's practice like a scientist having just discovered the cure for the common cold. I explained the plan to the players and had the team repeat our three rules in unison. Number one: No gaps between teammates; Number two: Stay low, hands and toes; Number three: When you make contact, lift them up with you.

Saturday morning came and standing in the team huddle they yelled back at me the rules of our new plan. We received the ball and players ran out of the huddle with new enthusiasm. The ball was hiked and the players on the line executed the rules perfectly. As a team they moved forward in the dirt with no gaps between them and as they made contact with the opposing team, they began to stand, lifting the other player up with them. The halfback was given the ball, and as he sprinted around the end, the stands full of sleeping parents began to come awake, coaches were screaming along the sidelines, video cameras were being unpacked. The runner was finally tackled thirty yards downfield; a run that tripled the total gain of the season.

We did not win any games that season, but we

learned some important things that stay with a person long after one game or one season is over. Stay in touch with teammates – no gaps! Sometimes you have to get dirty – stay low. When you make contact with the person in front of you, lift them up to as high as you are. I recall my friend's three rules for moving the ball on other fields and during other seasons.

Once I was asked to lead a church...

Stealing the Oranges – with permission!

Those orange trees that line the grassy mall in front of the Native America chapel at Cook College, Tempe, Arizona were just too full of fruit for their own good! No purple stamped SUNKIST on the peel, no chemicals added for color enhancement, but bite into one and the sweet meat releases a torrent of orange juice that runs down your chin, picking up speed to the wrist, until orange drops splatter the ground beneath bent elbows. I know they are that good because when I was there, I stood on tiptoe and picked a few each morning before breakfast. In a way, you could say I "stole" them. That is to say that I did nothing to produce the fruit. I took full and free advantage of the labor and time investment of someone else. Now it wasn't really stealing though. You see, I was given permission by some other people on campus to take from our host trees, but it wasn't the grower that said I could.

The sweetness that nourished me, refreshed me, awakened me, strengthened me for the 101-degree days I faced, was not something I earned. I didn't plant or cultivate or care. The orange gift was simply something

I received.

That morning became afternoon in the desolate desert reservation camp and church of Vah Ki with heat that sliced through Sunblock 85. But then, I could go to the ice chest and pull out the "stolen fruit" and feel strength enter a tired body again.

Before I left the reservation for the last time, I gave some of the fruit to my Pima friends at Vah Ki. Almost as if to compound my crime, I took what I didn't grow, even though with permission, and gave some away just because I thought they would like it.

So many joys, pieces of my life that shape me, nourish me, refresh me are the result of another's labor. In fact, most things I label "good" are just things that someone else shared with me.

The enormous tree in my grandparent's yard that gave birth to imaginary stories of Tarzan was not planted by me. The song that touches my soul and spins in my mind and makes me feel happy or sad or loved or lost was written and sung by a genius that was not mine.

It seems that so much of life is a constant sharing and borrowing, taking and receiving not what we have earned by our planting, but it is the fruit from another's labor. Yet, plant and cultivate and care we do; for there will be those who will steal the fruit from us with our permission.

The wisdom of a man named Jesus talks a bit about branches, vines and the fruit that is the produce. A book within the book speaks about "fruits of the Spirit" such as joy, peace, love, patience and the rest. But what the vine and I produce is not so much for my benefit but for someone else to consume. I produce fruit for another's table, just as another has filled mine. The Chinese have a proverb that says: "when eating bamboo sprouts, remember the man who planted them."

With every nightfall I can welcome the time of rest in gratitude because I have eaten my fill from the tree of life that I have not planted but that gives me life all the same...

When the world doesn't spin on my finger . . .

I feel drawn to water. I love its movement, its depth, its beauty, and its seeming power to calm the spirit, mind and body. That is why for a few days each September I stay in a small cabin at the waters edge to rest (kind of), reflect and re-gather myself. That is what I was doing at the lake, but it didn't look like it was going to be the kind of week I had envisioned when I had first made my plans.

I had a good friend from a city in which I used to live die after a short struggle with cancer over the weekend. I was honored when asked by his family to participate in the wake and prayer service and then the funeral on Monday and Tuesday. My friend had been an active parishioner in the Catholic Church, and the services were for a man of great faith and widely loved by people in the community and the Optimist Club, through which I had come to know him. My journey to the lake was delayed, and although I wanted to be with my friend's family, it subtracted a couple of days from my plans.

The reason I go to the lake after Labor Day is because it is less expensive but most of all because the summer

83

crowds have died down and I am used to having pretty much the run of the resort area to myself. It's much more quiet, less hectic and my accommodations are always at my choice. But, oh no, not this week! This turned out to be the week that couples and groups of those wanting to fish decided to show up and change my expectations.

First, I got stuck in the smallest and most cramped cabin, in the middle of the rest instead of down on the end where I could be by myself. It was also the only cabin that didn't have a front deck, where I like to sit and do my reading and writing. Next to me were not one or two but three couples staying together. While the men were fishing the women sat on the front deck, yelling back and forth to one another. On the other side was a 2 year old that was just old enough to be loud and able to run and outdistance his grandmother in a footrace to the water's edge.

As I sat in the only available lounge chair a few feet from the lakeshore, I began to put down my random thoughts about how I was displeased with my situation at the lake.

sitting...frustrated...wanted a bigger cabin – more room no people...quiet...
a boat for the day...no lawn mower...no telephone ringing...no car starts...
no interruptions   by friendly fishermen...
no giggling girls beyond girlhood years...
I...
deserve a deck out front for me!

But, the world doesn't spin like a basketball on the

index finger of my right hand. I get to live and enjoy life, and all the sounds of life. What more should I expect? What more could there be to enjoy?

Noise …of water slapping against the carved shore;
The raspy voice of a displeased duck;
White froth trailing behind the pleasure pontoon on its
Way through the water's channel pathways;

Laughter sprouting from seeds of friendship
Having survived journeys through slicing pain and
Punctuated silliness.
Gulls coasting on the unseen breath of God;
Diving, racing the catfish below for a dinner morsel…
Inviting each one to come and partake.

Just a couple of thoughts about my day at the lake, a gift from the One who separated the waters from the land…

Maybe A Dream

The sanctuary was filled with shadows created by early morning light creeping through the back windows —windows uncovered after several years of being closed by dust soaked drapes. It was a routine of many mornings; a time of quiet reflection, silent listening, a heart's communication with a spirit deep within me, returning to the One from whom it came. Some would call it meditation, or centering, pondering or maybe "just thinking." Someone might call it prayer. Whatever it's called, it is an important time of the day. Unhurried by busy-ness it is a time to reconsider just what all the busy-ness is for.

As I sat on the front pew, center row, almost within touching distance of the communion table, now empty except for the covers from bread plates and cup holders, the brick railing became a place to lay folded hands and a bowed head. The sound of an occasional creak of the roof was the only sound that interrupted the slowing rhythm and release of each breath.

While sitting in silence, to my mind came images of the church. There were days the room was empty and days it was full. People were singing and laughing. There were lively faces of people engaged in conversation of the heart and of the mind. The face in one of many caskets became vivid once again as well as the memory of family faces, courageously holding back tears that begged to be released to cascade down cheeks and lips.

Then, something happened. Someone might call it a vision, maybe imagination, the fragment of a dream, the leftovers of a movie watched or a painting visited. There, in my mind's vision, the cross. Upon the cross was hanging the nailed body of a man I knew as Jesus. His body was beaten, bruised, bloodied by the whips of those who had arrested and mocked him. It was not the Jesus of recent movie fame, because as much as his body was abused, there was something different about his face. The crown of thorns was in place. Wounds were visible on his cheeks but there was an indescribable serenity and power to his look.

It was not a look of beaten submission or helpless abuse. His was an expression of power. The eyes looked almost defiant but not really, because defiance has arrogance to it. I can only describe the look as one of power, unbelievable love and control.

The face from the cross looked at me, standing at its foot looking up. I wanted to hear him say something. In the moment, I wondered what words would come, if any, that would make sense to me. I wanted – I needed –to hear something for me.

Just two words came. They were said only once. They only needed to be said once because there was no lack of clarity. The voice from the cross simply said, "for you."

My voice does not have to be the same as another's to be true – it only has to be true. I can then quote myself with authority.

Belief Left Behind

Occasionally the idea shows up in a sermon about family relationships. Often the words are used as an instruction to the couple standing in front of the minister making pledges of marriage commitment to one another. They are words from the Bible and so they are considered more important than mere opinion. The couple is reminded that this is one of the moments in life in which they leave behind allegiance to parents and give their life allegiance to someone else.

Several years ago I began to include a greater emphasis on that change of allegiance in the wedding services I perform. The marriage couple is reminded that parts of the wedding service are a symbolic reminder of the pledge they make. The procession down the aisle is between rows of family and friends, but during the ceremony, the couple stands apart from them. The bride and groom stand closer to one another than to anyone else. The gathering of family and friends are still in the background, loving and supporting, but they are no longer the primary relationship.

Anyone who knows me or has read what I write or heard what I say would have no doubt of my love and respect for my mother and father. Each day I am thankful for the gifts of love and faith that I received from them. I am grateful for the foundation of belief that was the fertile soil in which the seed of my life was planted, tended and grew. But the water and sun of that growth was the expectation to think, consider, question and decide important things for myself. The reminder that there are times to *leave father and mother and cling to something else* is not only for weddings.

In order for a life of belief to be owned and authentic, there has to be some leaving of the parental belief behind. That leaving is not to say that family history of believing is of no value. It was that belief history that molded who I am now and allows and invites that leaving. Those cultural, political and religious beliefs were good, meaningful and valid for parents. They helped make sense in life that included World Wars, racism, economic depression, cotton fields and polio. They may not help make sense in life for me. To say, "leave the beliefs", even strongly held by mother and father, and cling to something else does not mean that those beliefs have no value. To leave says that perhaps those beliefs were incomplete.

Belief, whatever it may be, is situational. Belief may contain at best a portion of the *truth* that speaks to that moment. Therefore, because it is belief set in time, it is always partial.

I have stood in front of my sons and their brides at their weddings and heard those pledges of promise they made to one another. When I said those words to them about leaving their father and mother I was speaking to me as well. The reminder was not only for that wedding moment. The beliefs of others that have gone before me and I have loved might not now be all of the *truth* for me. I do not have to surrender all of my beliefs and I do not demand that others hold the exact same beliefs to be true. Sometimes I need a reminder that even what I believe as absolute, may not be enough of *truth* for them...

The search for God is a search for truth and as you can only find God as guided by God, you discover truth only as you are guided by truth.

Aloneliness

There is a desert of the spirit, parched and left barren by the hot winds that never cease to blow. It is a place where time and life do little more than exist. This is a desert in which nothing with color grows and there are no blossoms to be seen. It is a place through which I will sometimes journey and am fortunate to finally find an awaiting oasis. There is an end to my walk and once again I will feel the cool breeze of a still night promising the dawn of a new day. As the desert journey ends, I feel the soothing mist of the spring that bubbles with the sound of the human voice. In front of me are the courageous blades of new growth breaking through the crust of trampled sand and the skeletons of shriveled dreams. But, there are some stretches of time in which the journey seems to have no end and little hope of refreshment. It is a wasteland of "aloneliness."

Aloneliness is a completely different human experience than "aloneness." My aloneliness may be filled with people around me. Aloneliness is the emptiness that fills me. Aloneliness hears the sound of voices that are asking, demanding, expecting, wanting, needing, challenging, arguing, condemning and reminding of all that I am not and never will be.

Sometimes in moments of aloneliness all voices are for someone else; loving voices for anyone else.

In my aloneliness, others may be present, but there exists a ravine that separates any relationship of common ground upon which we each stand.

Aloneness is the emptiness that surrounds me. To be alone is to breath deeply of the silence until my spirit is filled with that silence alone. It is in that filling there is room enough to hear the whisper that is spoken to me alone. In the aloneness I am not required to respond to every voice simply because I hear its sound. In my aloneness, I may choose the voice I will hear and to only that voice will I respond. It is that voice, heard in my aloneness that reminds me who I am. It is the voice that invites me to drink deeply from the refreshing still waters. It is the voice that nudges me from the desert onto the fertile land where new life grows.

In my aloneliness a dreadful fear silently slips into my spirit; while in aloneness, strength to battle any fear can be discovered.

In my aloneliness I am empty of any sense of being loved; while in aloneness, I can hear the voice of the One who loves completely…

At the end of a search for a great motivation to spur me into energized action, I came to realize: It is not one great external event, but the everyday by everyday search to answer the question of the Psalmist and the Prophet, "Who am I?" and "What does God require of me today?"

The First Eight

Whether I want it, whether I dread it, whether I am ready for it, every morning it happens. After a night of restless waking up only to look over at the lighted green numbers on the alarm clock, new sleep has finally arrived. Those moments just before dawn are a time for mindless and dreamless existence. Into this best and most beautiful time comes a piercing sound that announces with the urgency of a fire truck barreling through a city intersection, time to begin my day. It is an announcement, a demand really, to toss back warm covers, swivel legs until they bend, and reach down to let feet touch the floor. But in this cry of the alarm's demand, there is also the possibility of grace. There is another gift of time.

Like most other alarm clocks, mine has a narrow plastic button on top. It is labeled with the name "Snooze" and if I press it or hit it, the alarm will grow silent and allow me eight beautiful minutes of blessing before sounding again. I am given the beautiful gift, a blessing of eight more minutes to enjoy not answering the call of the day. Those eight minutes are a gift with which I can do anything I choose.

Now, some people believe that eight minutes are not

enough time to do anything. Few lives will be changed, fortunes won or art works created in a mere eight minutes. But eight minutes is really just long enough to accomplish many wonderful things.

There was a few years that I traveled and did consulting work with organizations, including the church. On occasion, the church leadership would ask for an evaluation of the Sunday morning worship experience. During my times doing those evaluations, I discovered that in the first eight minutes after I exited my car and headed into the church, I had an opinion about the church. In the experiences of those first eight minutes I could determine if the congregation wanted and expected first time visitors and how a majority of the membership felt about their church. It was easy to determine what was most important to the congregation in eight minutes. And in those first eight minutes I knew how I was going to feel when the service was over and whether I would want to return.

Eight minutes, properly used, can accomplish many things. As Abraham Lincoln spoke at the dedication of a cemetery at Gettysburg, what he said took far less than eight minutes. A well-trained athlete can run over one mile and I can drive across my hometown in eight minutes. A person can propose a toast, a good idea, or even a marriage in less than eight minutes. I can turn a second cheek and say, "Please forgive me. I was wrong," in less than eight minutes. For doing some important things, eight minutes can be more than enough time.

Instead of trying to capture eight more minutes of sleep every morning, maybe I could use that "snooze time" as my daily goal setting time. I have come to believe that I need to have three goals for every day. I need to have an "easy goal." This can be any goal or intention that is not particularly hard to accomplish but needs to be done none-the-less. In fact, maybe just getting up is that goal. Every day I also need to have a "stretch goal." This is a goal or intention or plan that makes me reach a little beyond myself. It may mean trying something new or doing something a new way. My stretch goal is just that – it is a stretch for me. In order to accomplish my plan it will take effort. It will not only take effort, but will almost always take the input or help of someone else. And, every day should also include a "miracle goal." I would define a miracle goal as that intention or plan that I cannot accomplish without God being a part. How could my day change if my first eight minutes were spent finding my three goals for that day?

On most days, I am asked before leaving the house in the morning, "What are you going to do today?" It has always been a difficult question to answer because much of what I do is determined as I make my way through the day. On occasion, I have played around with my answer and announced that I was going end cancer, create world peace, run a sub-three minute mile, re-roof the church and learn to speak fluent Chinese. Usually I was the only one who found my answer amusing. So, I came up with a new answer that I hope is true every day. Today, I am going to "hang out with God, try to make a difference in someone's life, and have some fun." And, when I wake up in the morning, I have all of my first eight minutes to plan…

Because we are too busy to listen does not mean God is not speaking. Because we are too busy to notice does not mean that God is not present.

Raindrops and Waterfalls

I remember hearing a story about a seminary chapel service. One day, a few minutes before the daily chapel service was to take place, the faculty discovered that someone had removed all of the chairs. Since there was not time to round up others, everyone had to stand during the services. The seminary student, who was to speak that day, changed the mood in the room with his opening statement. He began, "I am looking forward to writing my mother about this. She will be thrilled to hear that when I preached today, every seat was taken and there were 400 people standing."

Most of the "good and bad" of our daily lives are created not by the situation or event itself, but by our approach dealing with it. That is not to say that there are not hurtful or disappointing things that happen around us. Life is not always as we would choose it to be. A man named Paul wrote a letter to an early church that had more than a few inconveniences with which to deal. He reminded them to find the positive things and focus on them. He did not ask them to be naïve and stick their heads in the sand. What he said was:

"If there is anything good, beautiful, life-giving; focus on these things."

    A man was once walking through a dense forest, trying to make his way home, several miles away. As he walked, a hard rain began to fall and even though it was dropping through the foliage of the forest, he could feel the rain pounding on his back and running down his neck. As he walked along, he became more and more discouraged. He tired and even began to complain to God about his unfortunate plight. Complaining soon turned into anger and he was ready to begin to curse God for creating the discomfort of his life, when he heard a noise coming from a clearing up ahead. As he entered the clearing, his eyes began to focus on a magnificent waterfall, cascading over the edge of a cliff over one hundred feet high, into a pool below. The rush of the falling water, the bubbling of the pool and the reflection of the water made the man smile. In the clearing, the man began to feel his fatigue become smaller, his breathing quieter and he was thankful for what he saw. A voice within him then reminded him that he had earlier cursed the drops of water falling from above that he now loved.
    I guess it is about what you focus on and what you see...

You have to have an appetite to know you are hungry but you can lose your hunger when you fill up with junk, leaving you starving to death and not knowing it.

Not the "est" Anything

It came as a shock to me. For one of the few times in my life, I really did not know what to say. I was unhappy that she said it and my ego was bruised more deeply than I like to admit. She was not trying to be mean or verbally hurtful, but she was one of those people who does not spend much time or effort in considering what someone else hears when the words are let loose. I could not disagree with her, but I still did not like to hear someone else say it.

She was standing in the church hallway, just outside the place where the children met for some of their activities. There was a conversation going on between her and one of the children's ministry leaders when I just happened to walk into her comments. She was telling the leader how disappointed she was in the opportunities for her children at the church. She also had some critical comments to make about the lack of communication between the church leaders and parents like her. They were both issues of which we were aware and she was right. Her next sentences were an explanation of her desire to continue as a part of the congregation even though most of her social and business friends went elsewhere. Then she looked at the church leader and at me and out came the words. "You know", she said, "this isn't the coolest church in town to be a part of!"

I could feel the cold steel sliding through flesh and between bones as the verbal knife was planted in my back. I wanted to jump on the moment and defend the church, us and me! What did she mean that we were not cool? Of course we were. All she had to do was ask anyone who regularly showed up for worship! Sunday morning services were filled with meaningful symbolism. Every service was filled with great music by singers and instrumentalists. Each sermon was a theological masterpiece. What did she mean we were not the coolest? My ego was deflated like a birthday balloon with a slow air leak.

I had always dreamed of being the "est" something while growing up. In my dreams, I was always the bigg*est* or fast*est* or smart*est* or strong*est* or just simply the b*est*. While there is nothing wrong with wanting and trying to be the "est" that I can be, there is a problem when all of life is approached as a competition with the world. Each day and every relationship can become a competition to prove my superiority over someone else. When that becomes my approach to the ministry of the church, a little thing called pride takes the place of humility and service.

I have lived long enough to realize that I am not ever going to be "est" when I compare myself with the rest of the world. So, with my ego somewhat in check, I began to think more clearly about what she had said. It was true that we were not the "est" anything when compared to other congregations in town. We were not the biggest, richest, newest, youngest, oldest, prettiest, or coolest. But maybe "est" is not what being faithful is about. I reminded myself that we were trying to simply be faith*ful*, hope*ful*, lov*ing*, serv*ing* and giv*ing*. In every way possible, we keep trying to be like the One, who is the "est" everything…

Never surrender the best part of yourself in a futile effort to be normal.

Everything But Dirt is Up

In the shadows of a night-covered room, a man sits. Alone and unmoving, he sits, staring out from an inner darkness that is blacker than any moonless night. The only sound is a quick gasp of breath that pierces the silence. Then comes an exhale of surrender that announces not only sagging shoulders but also, a sagging spirit.

Thoughts becoming visions play within his mind like a slideshow of disappointment. In that moment of life, nothing seems to matter. Self, others, accomplishment, task, challenge, love, life or even God makes any difference. However God is something to think about. He wonders if God is responsible for everything he is and feels and what in the world did God have in mind.

He wonders if the scene being played out on his life stage is his alone or are there others stages filled with other actors. Maybe the smile he sees in the morning just disguises for a little while the shadows still lingering inside. Religion tells him that stretched out before him is a promise, at least a hope or maybe a potential of a heaven. But, that is for later. What does God have in store for now?

Maybe it is helpful to return to the beginning. Maybe an answer can be found in an old, old story. If we remember and rethink the oldest faith story we have, maybe there we will find a clue.

I recall those words, "In the beginning..." using whatever method and timetable God thought was appropriate, God created all. The story then says that God took the dust of the earth and formed humanity. God shaped what is and breathed into it life and breath and after examining all that had been done, pronounced over it a benediction, "It is good!"

I read in another telling of the story that God took the humanity that had been created, picked it up and set it down in the midst of a garden created in beauty.

The story told does not propose to give a lesson in anatomy or biology. That is not what the story is about. In fact, the truth found in the story is much more important and life changing than that. I suppose that it could be said that God took a clod and with breath, made it human. I guess if I were to get a simple moral from the story, it would be, "without God, I am just an old clod." So, do I approach life like a clod, or a creation of God? The simple fact is that I started out as dirt so everything else is up!

There is real pain in life. There is real loss, real disappointment, real frustration and real tragedy. There is also the knowledge that everything but dirt is up.

In a friend's house, hanging on the wall next to the front door was a little shadow box. In that box there was a piece of wood on which was written, "I'm me and I'm wonderful because God don't make junk!" Remembering those words, whenever someone would ask me "How are you?" I would tell them, "I'm wonderful!" Even when they would shake their heads and start to laugh I knew the saying was more than humor or arrogance. It is a simple reminder of who you are in the midst of the mess.

Of course, someone will always ask, "But what about all the commandments? What about the do this and don't do that stuff?" They are there but they are not for God's benefit. All of those rules and commandments for my life are not to make God feel good. Neither are they a way for me to bargain for God's love. There is no pawnshop love from a pawnshop God. There is no trading or bargaining. They are a gift for my benefit because when I pay attention to them they make life best.

On my very, very worse day, I am not a clod. God has intentionally and lovingly formed me, shaped me and breathed that holy breath into my lungs. I am here because I was made out of the "want to" of God, who was pretty pleased with the way I started out. When I begin to remember that, I am not about to lie down, whimper and play dead.

When I begin to consider and really begin to understand the reality of what God has done, I am left simply to say "Wow!" I am not sure that it is a proper theological word but it should be. "Wow" is a shout that just has to be followed with "Thank you!" After all, I started out as dirt… everything else is up…

Sometimes going to church is like wandering through an enormous store in which everything is on sale, so you leave empty-handed because nothing seemed special and worth the cost.

The Jesus List

Maybe you saw it, too. Maybe you have seen it before since it is replayed on television every so often. It's the story of two men, both facing the rapidly approaching end of life who chose to spend their remaining time together, fulfilling a shared <u>Bucket List</u>. Portrayed by actors Morgan Freeman and Jack Nicholson, two men, one white and one black, embark on an adventure to fulfill a lifetime of dreams and accomplish what the everyday getting by of life had kept them from doing. It's a wonderful story that has invited lots of people, especially middle-age men, to write out a personal "bucket list" and start on a personal adventure of doing.

Like those other men of advancing years, I also began to again think about what I would put on my list if I knew that time was short and money was no object. But then, I began to wonder about what someone else would put on his bucket list.

Jesus knew the inevitability of the coming results of his life. Whether he knew the exact timetable or not, he heard the whispers of the authorities that stood around the fringes of the crowds that gathered to hear and see him. He knew that his words that called into question the integrity of the religious institution of his day and confronted the political power of Rome itself would lead him to a cross. He knew that you don't love the unlovable, forgive in the midst of the cries for judgment, and point out the least powerful as those cherished most in God's eyes without there being a price to pay. And, the greater the love – the greater the price. Jesus didn't wish to receive the cross, but he was willing to receive the cross if it was the price he had to pay for the life of love and truth that he lived as God's intention. So, I wonder, what would be on Jesus' "bucket list." If he had only a short while left, what would he choose as absolutely most important to accomplish? If he had time left for only a few words, what words would he share? If there were moments left for only a few acts of love, what would those acts be?

With an upper room, a cross and a tomb lying ahead, what do the last steps of the journey look like? I recall the stories of what he did the beginning of that last week after coming triumphantly into Jerusalem. I remember that he first went to the place where people worshipped and not turning his back on it, he powerfully reminded the crowd what God intended the place to be. He reminded those there doing business, looking out primarily for themselves and finding ways to limit someone else's closeness to God, that God's intention was that it be a place and time of relationship. It was created to be a place of connection and communication with God for all people. I remember a conversation Jesus had to make sure everyone understood what were the keys to life – love for God and love for others. I can see Jesus in an upper room having a meal with those he called friends, and he showed them that real power was also real humility and servanthood as he washed the dust from their feet. I hear again his prayerful words to God about willingness to go to a cross and death if that was God's intention even though it would not be his choice. Finally I can hear again the most powerful words ever spoken in human history when looking down from a cross on which he hung, came the words "forgive them..."

For many Christians, there is a time called Lent that is meant to be a time of personal reflection and preparation for the celebration that is to come. Lent is a time to consider deeply what is truly important in our life journey. If redirection is needed, it is a time to make those journey adjustments. It is a time to exhume gifts buried out of fear and begin to invest them in the way God intended when they were first given. This is a time to compare our bucket list with Jesus' and wonder if one reflects the other.

I think I need to do a bit more work on mine...

Faith is the power within that gives us backbone and voice. It is reflected in everything we do and are. It gives direction to our steps and meaning to every decision. Faith is not our possession but it is that which possesses us.

A Noose in the Family Tree

Someone once observed that the bad thing about studying your family tree is that you may accidentally discover someone "hanging" on it. That is a good way to remind ourselves that it is not always safe to rely on our illustrious ancestors to give us status in life. It is even more foolish to believe that we are the only family with an embarrassing or humiliating experience to live down. We are not the only family with a black sheep grazing under the family tree.

I grew up hearing stories about my great-great grandfather. They were stories about his courage in standing up for what he believed. Listening to the telling of family story and history, he always looked like a hero to me.

At the beginning of the American Civil War, my great-great grandfather was a newly wed, living in Kentucky with his family. As a blacksmith and farmer, he worked hard to make a life for his new bride and himself. As the War Between the States began, young men from the area were enlisting in the Army of the Confederacy. He, too, was expected to enlist to fight for the South. This is where the story begins its heroic adventure. The way the story was told by the family was how he felt the wrongness of slavery and could not, in good conscience fight to preserve its hold on the American way of life. Therefore, he left his home in Kentucky and traveled to Indiana, leaving his family and heritage behind. Once in Indiana, he enlisted in the Union Army, to fight against what he saw as a social wrong and national tragedy. To this very day, he is listed as a "traitor" in that little hometown in Kentucky.

That is the way I heard that story growing up. His heroism in the face of social and political turmoil was to be admired. That is the kind of story that you use for writing assignments submitted in middle school. The problem showed up after I grew to be an adult and I heard the rest of the story.

After arriving in Indiana in the fall, he enlisted in the Union Army to fight for the preservation of the United States. However, when springtime arrived, he was tired of being a soldier and he wanted to go back to farming. So, my "heroic" great-great-grandfather deserted from the Union Army, went home to farm and later left Kentucky to make his way out west to Texas and Oklahoma. My great-great-grandfather has the unique position of being listed as a "traitor" to the South and a "Deserter" to the North.

We honor and remember with special holidays men and women of courage who have made sacrifices of life and well being for others. We should do that. But, I am afraid that in what appears to be an attempt to inspire others to a life of courage, sacrifice has become a game and heroism an easily tossed around title.

Conflicts are not settled by plastic 12 inch high figures dressed in camouflage and purchased from a local department store. Real courage is not found in playing an electronic game in which "body count" starts back at zero with the flick of a switch. Sacrifice is not a game played out on television between teams of contestants in battle gear for the vicarious entertainment of the armchair audience.

Those who rightfully carry the name hero are not those who wish for the conflict or look forward to the stench of battle. For them it is no game to be enjoyed or glorified. It is not a wish but a willingness to give completely of themselves to something or someone beyond self that makes them what they are. We who sit and watch and are entertained as if they are contestants on a world-sized football field, dishonor them and all who have served before them.

Real heroism, service and love that sacrifices is not about wishing but being willing…

I cannot point to another's selfishness as permission for my own.

Someone Ruined My Christmas

In the middle of all the excitement and fun of this once a year holiday, the grumbling begins. Christmas music entertains shoppers as they wander or sprint up and down store aisles in search of the "perfect gift." The aromas of fresh baked cookies, cakes, pies and fattening treats of every taste and description make their way from oven to tabletop to waistline. Lights are hung from houses and trees, or at least re-straightened if they never made it down after last years celebration. Tongues are tired and hands exhausted from signing, addressing Christmas card greetings to people you haven't connected with for the past 11 months and 25 days.

Oh, but that's not all. This is also that time of year that politico-religionists begin their own holiday journey of complaints. They complain that nativity scenes are not allowed on courthouse lawns. They groan that Christmas carols with Christian themes are not allowed to be sung in schools and a national decorated tree has been referred to as a "holiday tree" instead of the traditional "Christmas tree." In fact to listen to some of these complaints, a person would be led to believe that my faith and celebration of the biblical story of the birth of God's son in Bethlehem would be destroyed because of these failures on the part of society and government to support that faith.

Oh Humbug!!

There are times that I long for a past when celebrating Christmas was simpler, less commercialized and didn't begin until after Thanksgiving. But is my faith and celebration so fragile that if my government and society and schools and television and Wal-Mart don't help me out, that my faith will shrivel up and blow away?

It was when this life-changing commitment to be a disciple of the one we proclaim as God's Son and the Christ became too officially aligned with the government of the day (300 years after Jesus) and faith became not only accepted but also expected, that faith began to dwindle and lose much of its rich power. Maybe Christmas is the time to remember that we are disciples of one who was born in a stable, as an outcast, sought from his birth by the political, religious, social and cultural power of that day so he could be destroyed – not supported. Maybe it's good to remember that those same powers did not celebrate his birth or his life and eventually nailed him to a cross. Maybe we need to remember that those first disciples of Jesus were persecuted by the powers of their day because they held themselves to a higher allegiance.

If I find myself disheartened that no nativity is found on the courthouse lawn, perhaps I should build one on my front lawn. If I am afraid that the school's rule to not sing Christian Carols will keep my children from having faith, perhaps I need to teach them myself.

Perhaps it is actually my responsibility to tell them the story of Bethlehem and live my parental faith every day so they learn that the Bethlehem birth still makes a bigger difference in life than accomplishments on a sports field or court. If I am concerned that Christ is being taken out of Christmas, it may be possible that I could invite someone into the house who has his name over the door and tells his story every week.

Just maybe the only one who can keep Jesus as the "reason for the season" is me…

There is no one all-inclusive procedure to guide all of life. Even to say "love always" cannot be codified, but really says many things. Even Jesus spoke of a great commandment of behavior above all else but then lived it in many expressions. The experience of living shapes the response.

So Many Boxes

Boxes!

So many boxes. . . covered with bright shiny paper, rainbows of color neatly tied in ribbons and bows, just waiting for young and not so young to rip and tear and discover the wonders inside. Little boxes are cardboard and tape treasure chests holding the secrets of childhood, buried in a special spot in the yard, beneath the big tree, a spot known only by a handful of the very best of friends. Boxes!

There are so many boxes. A tiny velvet box, holding crystals of sparkling beauty, is offered on bended knee as a lifetime proposal and promise. Boxes!

So many boxes to hold the lives of people making sure they fit into our plan and design. You need to begin to act your age. Grow up. Big girls and boys don't do that. You are too young. You are too old. Boxes! Gender boxes tell us "that's man's work. That's a woman's job. Little girls shouldn't do that. Little boys don't act that way." Boxes!

Sunday mornings and Wednesday nights are stacked with so many boxes of religious absolutism. "A real Christian doesn't believe that, say that or do that." If it's not my way, it must be the wrong way. Boxes!

Everywhere you look there are so many boxes labeled age, sex, color, race, belief, lifestyle, politics, status, and religion. Boxes!

For his whole life, even those who followed and knew him best tried to find the box into which Jesus would fit.
"Jesus, good people don't hang around people like that." Boxes!
"Jesus, how many times should I forgive? I need to pray for them?" Boxes!
"Jesus you can't do that healing today, it's the wrong day. You have to wait until tomorrow?" Boxes!
"You're going to whose house and having dinner Jesus?" Boxes!
"Jesus that's not what a Messiah would do or look like. Jesus, you can't go to Jerusalem and take the chance of being arrested and killed." Boxes!
"Jesus, stand up. You are the Christ. You are not supposed to wash my feet." Boxes!
"Jesus, you're dying on a cross. That's not what the Son of God would do. What's that you say about forgiving those who still hold the quivering hammer in their hand?" Boxes!

And finally, all the religious, social, political, military, cultural combined power of his day, found a box in which they could put him. A box chiseled from the rock on the side of a hill would be his final box. To make sure that this stone box works, they even put a stone boulder in front to cap it off.

The final box!

And a few days later, in the predawn darkness and chill, the only sound is the crunch of footsteps up a narrow path as some women make their way slowly to the tomb. As they arrive at the front of the stone box...

The gospel is not a collection of information, but a life that echoes the beat of God's heart.

As Simple As This

Sometimes you can hear them long before you see them. Driving along a country road, listening through the westward windows from the kitchen, sometimes even drowning out the music of the latest CD slipped into the slot in the dashboard comes the unmistakable sound of the geese. Migrating from south to north and back again, a favorite stopping place seems to be the leftover cornfields and farm ponds of northwest Missouri. You can see them swarming like bees around a hive. Huge formations of Canada Geese and sometimes the beautiful Snow Geese eventually swoop to the ground covering the field like a fresh blanket of snow.

I would presume that everyone has heard the stories, devotional and scientific about the geese flying in their famous "V" formation. But, a few years ago, I heard something that was new to me. While looking at the flying wedge formation, a friend of mine noted that one leg of the "V" was always longer than the other. He asked me if I knew why that was. After some thought and rummaging through my memory of all the goose formation stories I had ever heard, I had to admit that I had no idea why one leg of the "V" was longer than the other. My friend smiled and said simply, "because it has more geese in it." Duh! Looking for something complicated and profound, I overlooked the obvious and simple.

Whenever I approach the celebration of Easter, the story of Jesus from cross to tomb, I recall all the theological, historical, sociological, psychological explanations that I have heard throughout my lifetime. I recall the language of atonement, sanctification, justification, substitutionary sacrifice, transformational imagery and books from libraries filled with the explanations of brilliant men and women throughout Christian history. I wonder, if it's all not a little bit simpler than that. I wonder if maybe the power, beauty and meaning of Easter are not found in its complexity but its profound simplicity.

Into the middle of humanity at its worst with hammers still quivering in the soldiers' hands, nail spikes scattered on the ground with a man's clothes divided among his murderers and curses of disbelief spit from bitter lips, the Son of God chooses to die rather than surrender the message of God's love for those cheering beneath him. Into the middle of humanity at its worst, the words heard from the one on the cross are simple words of forgiveness.

A few hours later, some emotionally drained former followers make their way through the pre-dawn darkness toward a closed tomb. The man from the cross has been taken for burial and their hope and joy has been buried with him. As they walk they question one another about who has the strength to move the stone that covers the entrance to the tomb. Into the middle of humanity at its weakest, most powerless, into this powerlessness and death God moves in power to bring life.

Maybe the Gospel, the Good News, at its heart is God at God's best in the middle of us at our worse. Maybe, it is just that simple...

Faith is...
Down when I jump up,
Sound when the air is still,
Dawn as the sun settles into darkness,
The cool of the stream when I hear the raindrop,
The healing kiss while the scrape on my knee still burns.

Into the Shadow

We prefer light over dark; clear sight over the dim view from the shadows. Jesus is the light of God, the light of the world, the light of life, the light that shines in the darkness. But, there are moments, few though they may be, when the dark wields its power and seems in that moment to overwhelm the light. Tonight is a time like that. It is a temporary time that we know will not last, but it is here all the same.

These are the moments that come before the dawn. These are the moments that stand at the edge of the light. These are the moments when the shadows push against the light, trying to hold it away, but the shadows can only exist where there is the promise and presence of the light.

We remember the journey of Jesus from his magnificent entry into the city, hailed as conqueror and king, cheered by the voices of children and old, questioned by the faithful and the doubtful. It is a journey that takes us from the brightness of the day into the shadows of an upper room, of a garden, the shadow of crosses on a hillside outside the city and the hollow shell of a tomb carved out of the rock. This night, we not only remember but we also journey beside Him, into the shadows. We follow with our minds as we recall the stories. We follow with our eyes as we look at the symbols that still speak to us this night. We follow with our hearts as we recall that this – all of this is for us. We journey into the shadows, looking for the dawn.

There is a shadow at the table...

Moses took off his shoes when he knew he was on holy ground. He heard the voice he knew to be God. The voice spoke of a promise that the people would leave their slavery behind and be finally truly free. With fear and faith together, he went ahead of the people and led them to the edge of not just a land but a life of promise.

Around a table, on this special night, sit families who recall and retell that story of God's promise. These are people who live on the soil of God's promised place but are still held by slavery's chains. They are held by hunger for a food that is more than bread. They are held by old traditions that cry out "an eye for an eye . . . God will love only the few . . . someday a Messiah will appear and will rule like David, the king of the past."

The question is asked in the shadows, "Why do we eat this meal?" The well-known and always repeated answer comes. It is an answer about what God has done! One by one the bowls are passed and the food eaten and the story is remembered and retold. God has done great things!

Jesus sits at the table, surrounded by a family he has chosen. These are those common men who have heard his invitation to follow and left the life chained to the past and followed Him into a new life. But this night, they have followed Him into shadows.

He called them friends and reminded them of the life they shared together. These friends – fishermen, tax collector, shopkeeper, political radical – were left speechless as he slipped off his coat, bent onto his knees and began to untie sandals so that he could wash their feet.

In the moments when their time together should be ending, he invited them deeper into the shadow but closer to the light. He picked up the piece of bread left untorn, pulled it apart and gave it to them, saying, "This is my body. Eat!" He then reached across the table and picked up the bowl of wine, filled it again to overflowing, and gave it to them, saying, "This is my blood. Drink!"

As they ate and drank, the shadow would have been unbearable, except that they were at the table with their friend. This is the man that one of their group had begun to call the Chosen One. This one who was with them talked not just about what God had done in the past or even what God would do someday but what God was doing right before them.

Eat . . .
Drink . . .
Remember . . .

There is a shadow at the cross...

The cradle, formed and held together by nails and braided chord, held a crying newborn child. He was born to a mother and father, only partially his own, in a strange place, surrounded by the first acts of creation. The descendants of animals that witnessed the first creation of humanity are now the first watchers as God creates anew in a Bethlehem stable. Flickering candles cast shadows onto the face of the child and soiled shepherds.

Flickering torches cast shadows onto the face of the child- now a man and the face of a ruler still groggy when awakened from a midnight stupor. Within the shadows a crowd screams that death is the only solution for their desires of this night. A few questions, a few words in reply, a debate about power and the winner will be decided on a cross. With no easy choice within the reach of the one who decides, a man is dragged into the shadow where taunts grow and pain cuts into flesh and death awaits his arrival.

A cross, formed and held together by nails and braided chord, now holds a man who cries to feel God close by, shares a spoken moment of compassion with a thief who deserves none, and a mother and friend needing to lean on one another. He looks down through sweat and blood that fills his eyes at armed men who still hold hammers in calloused hands, but he screams no curse of anger or promise of revenge. In the shadow, as the sun darkens at mid-day, a prayer is whispered "Father, forgive . . ."

Forgive? Is that what he prayed?

Forgive? I don't believe that could have been it!

Forgive? We must have misunderstood!

Forgive? No one forgives when they are treated like this!

Forgive? What about "an eye for an eye?"

Forgive? How many bloody cheeks does he have left to turn?
Forgive? NO!
Forgive? NEVER!
Forgive? NOT EVER!
Forgive us our trespasses…
As we forgive…
Those who trespass…
Against me…
Against me…
Against me…

There is a shadow at the tomb…

It is dark in the middle of the day. That's not when the dark is supposed to arrive. The dark feels like a time to be afraid. The dark feels like a time to be so very alone. The dark is that time that there is no light seen at the end of a road. The dark is for the moment when life is completed, everything is done, plans are fulfilled.

It is dark in the middle of the day. The middle of the day is for the journey to continue together. There is more road to travel. There are more adventures to share. There is so much more to anticipate and plan. There has not been time enough to know all that can be known. The dark is not supposed to be in the middle.

It is dark in the middle of the day. There had been so much more to hope for. Hope that he was the one to redeem the world. Hope that all of life would now be different, better, changed. Hope that he would be with us until the end of the world. Hope that he would be at our table for every meal. Now, in the middle of hope and plans and dreams, the dark has come.

He was too young…
He had so much to live for…
Who knows what he could have become…
It is just not right!
Why didn't God do something?
If there was a God…

The faint light of the night, not so bright as a star that shown in the east resting over the place where a baby lay, flickers on the rock walls of a cave. Shadows hover in crevices where a great stone lays against the outer edges of the tomb's doorway.

The pathway winding up the hillside is dark and sharp rocks wait to impale the sandal and soul of anyone invading the shadows. It is much too steep a path to walk in the dark. This is too dark of a journey to take alone.

If the tomb is his destination, it must be ours too. We will go later. He asked us to follow. Does that mean into the shadow that hides life? Just before dawn, we will go toward the shadow – toward the tomb.

When the dawn comes, we will see…
When the morning comes, we will see…
When the sun rises, we will see…

Faith is not some object to be found and then lost with the hope of finding it again. Faith is life itself. It is the order and direction of life. Faith is the meaning and movement of life.

What God Won't Do

These past few months have been a strange collection of experiences for many. Record breaking heat and drought have parched large areas of the U.S. southwest reminding some of the "Dust Bowl" days of the past. Meanwhile, tornadoes have devastated areas from Missouri to Alabama and as far north as New York, while floods have been the results of Hurricane "whatever you name it." Fires have raged throughout western forests and flood waters released from swollen rivers in the north have washed away crops and fields up and down the Missouri River. Then you can add to that growing list, the hail and wind that left many small hometowns and the surrounding areas an insurance adjuster's nightmare. Put all together, weather announcers (you can call them forecasters or experts if you want), insurance companies and Main Street conversationalists lump it all into a category of events we call "Acts of God."

I just will not believe that God, at whim, decides to arbitrarily send destruction into my life. And, in spite of what a few misguided "religionists" may try to tell me, the events of September 11 were not the acts of a God bent on punishing the country for its acceptance of our common humanity regardless of sexual orientation or voting preferences. But at the same time, I pray to God to somehow be a part of my life in the midst of difficulty and have faith that the One to whom I pray will make a difference. Much of the time, I ask to be rescued or "saved" from the painful experiences of life.

My thinking and praying has led me to a list. This is a list of *What God Won't Do!* I do not think God chooses not to do these things because of meanness or inability. I believe if God rescues me constantly, plucking me out of the fires for which I sometimes stack the kindling, I am denied the freedom with which I am created. Just because God does not rescue me from events, God's Spirit and presence does make all the difference in that event. So, here's the list:

1. God will not rescue me from pain, but God will rescue me from hopelessness.
2. God will not rescue me from failure, but God will rescue me from fear.
3. God will not rescue me from empty pockets, but God will rescue me from an empty heart.
4. God will not rescue me from conflict, but God will rescue me from anger.
5. God will not rescue me from work, but God will rescue me from slavery to it.
6. God will not rescue me from searching, but God will rescue me from being lost.
7. God will not rescue me from loss, but God will rescue me from meaninglessness.
8. God will not rescue me from dying, but God will rescue me from despair.

I know that others, much more expert about "God things" than I may not agree with my list. Maybe they are right, maybe not. What I know is that this is the God that I believe in and loves me…always…

It is not the preacher's choice to decide if the crowd is large enough, ready enough and faithful enough to receive the message. God is large enough, ready enough and faithful enough.

Deep Water

I guess you could say that they really weren't anyone's neighbors. A person could talk to folks up and down the street and no one knew anything about them. There may have been some children in the family but they were never heard or seen playing in the yard. There were no names on the sports-pages in the local newspaper proclaiming one accomplishment after another. No one knew for sure what he did for a living except that he left early each weekday morning and arrived back after dark. His job apparently did not include weekends since the Sunday paper was always in the drive until mid-morning and then it disappeared. None of the local gossips knew whether she belonged to any clubs, leaving those neighbors most usually in-the-know without any good stories to tell. It is a place where the water runs deep.

To call it an old car would be generous. The beat up four-door had a bent coat hanger for a radio antenna, trunk tied down with baling wire and faded paint competed with rust in a race around the metal shell. The owners parked it at home down in the river bottom trailer park. This was no landscaped mobile home park.

These were just plain trailers with the replacement plywood floors beginning to split and bend under the weight of a growing ten year old. All of the family's money went to bills already overdue and perhaps a lottery ticket each week for the chance to hit it big just once. It is a place where the water runs deep.

The young couple never really even thought much about God except as the first half of a phrase spit out in anger. Not only did the language they use leave a bitter residue in the air, but also there was almost an aroma of profanity in the way they carried themselves. It is a place where the water runs deep.

He used to go all the time. While growing up there were always mission meetings, Sunday morning, Sunday night, Wednesday night and weeklong revivals out at the city park. The only television shows watched with enthusiasm had religious songs at the beginning, a sermonic promise for good things coming to you if only you gave to the program first. "Praise the Lord" punctuated every spoken paragraph. But then he just got tired of it all. All of the music, the words and the promises seemed to make no real difference. The religious folks he heard all seemed to be more interested in bank accounts, and love began to sound more like a financial plan. It is a place where the water runs deep.

Jesus and the boys were fishing. As he looked from the boat where he sat, he saw others who had fished through the night. When he saw the scattered carcasses of a few lake trout, he asked, "How's the fishing?" It had been a pretty mediocre day for fishing. They had done their fishing in the safety of shallow water close to shore.

Deep water is a little scary. You do not know what you might bring up out of deep water. All kinds of mysterious creatures live in deep water. The sea monsters like the one that swallowed a man named Jonah live in deep water. Storms that would quickly blow down from the hills with little warning would leave little time to retreat back to the safety of land and shallow water.

Jesus invites the men to try again and this time go to where the water runs deep. The results were miraculous. He then invites them to go deep-sea fishing with him.

Clubs are a gathering of people of similarity. Jesus was not recruiting for a club. Political action committees are a gathering of people with similar likes and dislikes. Jesus was not establishing a PAC. He invited all kinds of people to be disciples and it was a gathering of variety.

It is Jesus' nature and intention to go where the water runs deep. His fishing trip of living would take him into the homes of tax collectors, lepers, the poor, fishermen, zealous political radicals, the blind, and into the temple of religious tradition and into the lives of people not allowed into that temple. And, those who choose to follow him are invited to go fishing with him, where the water runs deep…

Wisdom is a moment's awareness following a lifetime's wondering.

Where To Fish

I met another man once who grew up with an acquaintance with Christian church people and church things. It was a Christmas-Easter kind of relationship. After graduating from high school and leaving his parent's house, he spent some of his adult years searching for something of meaning. He looked in many places for an understanding of the world, other people, and himself. He looked for some way of belief that would put him on a path toward God. The man explored all the great religions of the world and philosophies of the ancient world and the new age.

After many years of searching, the man returned to the place where his search had begun. He explained his arrival at the doorstep of Christian faith by talking about fishing. He said, "I walked along the banks of the lake and looked at all the places others were throwing in their lines. I saw all the places where I could fish. I watched people fishing in all the different spots and talked to them about how to fish. I decided to stop and fish where I saw others catching something…"

The use of a talent is like giving to the parent the picture that is drawn and colored with the crayon given to the child as a birthday present.

I Only Saw a Tree

I only saw the tree,
Crooked, gnarled limbs, winding their way through
The air like streams of water
Unbounded by a planned shoreline.

Its surface, covered by wooden warts,
Fractures of where limbs had once hung,
Once strong branches
Now unable to withstand the weight of a raindrop.

Once great and green, now paled by too many days,
Too many snows, too many storms
Drained of the color of life,
I only saw the tree.

I only saw the tree.
You, the craftsman, the artist,
You saw what lived within,
Untouched, untried, waiting to be set free,
In your hands creation began once again

Rough hands smooth the pale skin
And with gentle touch shape, carve, hollow, press
What was emptied of life begins to come to life
Arisen in color the shape on the mantle awaits
The gift of time.

Now the hands of the watchmaker, alive with
Anticipation
Put into order those unseen works awaiting a final
Touch
The touch, a twist, a turn and the rhythm of time
Begins.
I only saw a tree.

I only saw a man,
Stooped and bent, pale and weakened
By too many days, too many snows, too many storms
You saw the waiting to be set free.

In your hands, creation began once again.
I only saw a tree.

(Written for the funeral of an old craftsman who loved to make mantle clocks using discarded pieces of tree limbs. As the verses were being written, it became something much more.)

It is not my responsibility to convince people that I love them, but to love them.

These Hands

I heard a story once about a grandmother who was drawing a young woman's attention to her hands. I was reminded how a carpenter named Jesus was often recognized by his hands and the ways he used them.

The old grandmother asked the younger person, "Have you ever looked at your hands? I mean really looked at your hands?" As I heard the old woman's words, I stopped and looked carefully at my own hands and remembered. In a children's Sunday School class many years ago, we were drawing around one another's hands and after making an outline of mine the child loudly announced that I had "werewolf hands" because of the hair on my fingers. I took a moment and looked at my hands.

With these hands, I have touched and been touched by life. These hands have held tightly onto chairs and parent's hands as I took my first wobbling steps. These hands have reached out to steady my journey. Throughout the years, in the many ways I have fallen, these hands were grabbed and held by another's hands. By these hands, someone else has pulled me up until I was standing straight again.

These hands have dressed me in the styles of the day trying to be accepted by classmates and combed hair from shoulder long brown thickness to thinning gray. These hands have knotted a colorful multitude of ties not only around my own neck but those of sons and nervous grooms waiting their moment with a beautiful bride.

These hands have pushed lawn mowers, sacked thousands of groceries, and hung tightly onto the steel ladder of a barreling boxcar. They have opened doors, closed doors, slammed doors, rebuilt doors, unhinged doors and quietly opened a door to peek into the bedroom of a sleeping child. These hands have held a gun pointed at the heart of another human being and they have held the long stem of a red rose given to a lover.

These hands have felt the twin seams of lacing across a baseball as it was launched toward a crouching teammate. They have moved across the hands of a youngster, placing smaller hands across those same seams to guide another pitch to a batter three decades younger.

These hands have gripped a bat, felt the sting of a foul and been wounded by fishhooks, splinters, knives, kite string, campfires and hammers. These hands have been dirty, bruised, broken and now tremble out of control but they are the hands that have held newborn sons and grandchildren. They have held the head of a dying friend and the broken body of a stranger. They are the hands that stroked the cheek of a father and mother after their last breath was taken.

These hands have held a pen to record in word the

attempt to make God's presence and love known, celebrated and alive; and they have scratched out a thousand clumsy attempts.

In the words of the grandmother, "These hands are the mark of where I've been and the ruggedness of life."

Even now, I take a moment to look and listen to the story told by my hands…

• • •

By the way...

The question seems to be asked in almost every conversation I have with people I have just met. They discover that I am a minister but that I used to be a police detective. Then the question comes. With a perplexed look on the questioner's face, the question is asked, "How did you get from law enforcement into ministry? That seems like a pretty big change."

I wish I could say that one night while deep in prayer, God appeared to me and told me to change professions. I could say that once when I was working undercover I was attacked and beat up by three criminals and God miraculously helped me out of the danger. As I vividly remember that night God's name did come up while I was fighting but it was not in a prayer or in a bargain. The person asking the question might understand more if I could describe a wondrous "lightning out of the sky" experience. The decision really was about none of that. The answer is much more simple for me to know than for them to understand.

Yes, I had grown up in the church with people who tried to live out their beliefs. A few adults had told me that I should become a minister. But I had floated in and out of church involvement as I grew older and the choice became mine. In college, church attendance became a cheap date with less cost than dinner and a movie. The church had little attraction and the professional ministry had little excitement.

Maybe it was because of my relationship with someone who shared moments of life with me. Maybe it was a handful of words that I read somewhere that lit some flame within my mind. Maybe it was an expression of someone's belief that colored my life experience in a little different way. Maybe it was some of all of these.

Simply put, I guess I couldn't say "No" to the nudge anymore...

Thank You!

After many years of "planning to" write this book, its completion is the result of the helpful nudges of many people. I am grateful to Robert Dees, Spiritual Life Associates, for his commentary and encouragement throughout this journey and to Jennie Lamb who read and edited through every story. And, thank you to those who waded through my early attempts to put into print stories that had only been verbally shared. Most especially, I am grateful to the special people who throughout their lives have shared a moment with me that became a place where my life met love.

www.ingramcontent.com/pod-product-compliance
Lightning Source LLC
Chambersburg PA
CBHW051801040426
42446CB00007B/460